How to use

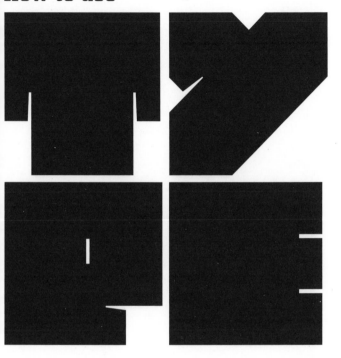

How to use

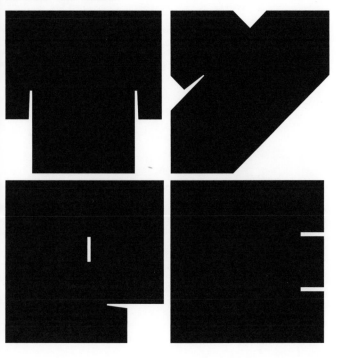

Lindsey Marshall & Lester Meachem

Laurence King Publishing

Published in 2012
by Laurence King Publishing Ltd
361–373 City Road
London EC1V 1LR
Tel +44 20 7841 6900
Fax +44 20 7841 6910
Email: enquiries@laurenceking.com
www.laurenceking.com

This book was produced by Laurence King Publishing Ltd,
London

A catalogue record for this book is available from the
British Library.

ISBN-13: 978 1 85669 897 9

Design: Jon Allan, TwoSheds Design

Typefaces: Vitesse, Forza, and Dox

Picture research: Emma Brown and Lindsey Marshall
Printed in Hong Kong

Related study material is available on the Laurence King
website at www.laurenceking.com

Special thanks to:

All those who contributed images, in particular Martin
Woodtli, Fons Hickmann m23, Happy Centro, André Apel,
Jan Schöttler, Thomas Pavitte, Yani Arabena, Guille Vizzari,
and Mission Design for the case studies. Thanks to John
Seth Marshall for the photographs.

Thanks to those at Laurence King who made this possible:
Helen Rochester for her vision and confidence in us, our
editor Anne Townley, also for her confidence in us and for
her forbearance, support, experience, and insight in
guiding us through the process. Likewise Clare Double for
seeing us through the final stages of publication.

Thanks to our partners Mike and Carol for continuing
support and patience (even more lunches prepared by
Mike). This book is dedicated to them.

Contents

Introduction

This book is intended as an introduction to the use of, and experimentation with, type in design for print and screen. It aims to provide creative, informative, and practical guidance in this essential aspect of visual communication. In order to achieve this objective, there will be a strong visual element drawing on a range of sources, which will reflect cultural diversity. After using this guide, the reader will have a grasp of how to use and—more importantly in the context of the book—experiment with type for a range of applications and contexts, both in print- and screen-based work. As well as giving clear instruction, the book is also intended to be a source of inspiration and a reference handbook.

The various chapters incorporate the fundamental principles and terminology relating to type, before examining how to select appropriate typefaces and lay them out effectively, and how to approach the design process: generating ideas, handling traditional and digital tools, communicating the message, using color and movement, and tackling production issues. There is a section specifically devoted to experiments with type, but this theme will be woven through the book supported by case studies, projects, and exercises.

Marian Bantjes has taken a playful approach to this poster design for an Australian winery. The names of all the winery's growers have been rendered in hand-drawn lettering on a dot matrix composed of different varieties of grapes, again drawn by hand.

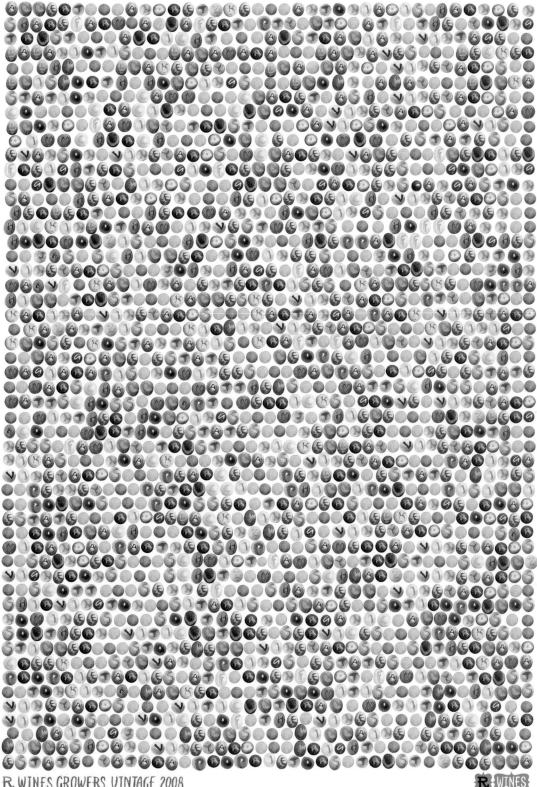

R. WINES GROWERS, VINTAGE 2008

R. WINES

What is type?

Although this book is not about designing a typeface, it is useful to have an understanding of the historical and technological context in which type has evolved.

Letterforms developed as an alternative means of communication to the spoken word. Initially this visual communication took place through pictograms, which use an image to represent an object, and ideograms, which convey more complex meanings such as actions.

These symbols gradually evolved, in different ways within different cultures and societies, into the letterforms we are familiar with today. The letterforms would originally have been hand-produced by scribes, but, with the increase in populations and need for more complex communication, mechanical means of producing the written word were developed. Woodcuts and woodblocks were used extensively to communicate one message to many people, for example, religious block books used by preachers.

In 15th-century Germany, Johannes Gutenberg revolutionized the way we communicate by developing movable type—type where letterforms were cast in multiples of individual characters so that a printer could put together letters into a series of words for printing and then reuse the type blocks for another text. This is the origin of what we know as type. Prior to this the written word was produced either calligraphically or by woodblock prints (opposite, above left and right). Gutenberg's system allowed for printing of letterforms quickly and economically, which meant that many more people were given access to the written word, leading to an increase in literacy. This method of printing type (generally known as letterpress) persisted, with modifications, well into the 1970s, when digital technologies began to transform type production. One of the characteristics of metal type is the debossing or indentations caused by the pressure of the type on the paper. This does not normally feature in digitally produced type unless a separate process is applied to simulate the effect. Designers often replicate

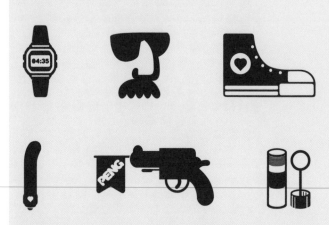

This series of dingbats by HVD Fonts includes pictograms, some of which may also be used as ideograms. For example, the pictogram of a watch may also be interpreted as an ideogram for time.

This store frontage has survived in its original format with 1950s-style design and contrasting use of typography.

letterpress or, where they can get access to appropriate equipment, will use letterpress to create specific effects, as in the examples shown on page 10.

As technological developments have improved methods of communication, the way we produce type has changed, so that today we can reproduce most letterforms for mass consumption, including simulated letterpress type. Therefore, throughout this book, when we refer to type we are using the term to describe any letterform, be it printed, inscribed, drawn, digitally produced, or modeled. Communication is normally the purpose of using type, whichever method of production is used.

clockwise from top: This example of an early hand-produced, one-off manuscript shows the way hand lettering was combined with images to communicate the message. Occasionally, and particularly with religious subjects, such manuscripts were laboriously copied for dissemination to the population.

A woodblock print could be used to produce multiples, but was limited in that, once created, it could not be changed.

These pieces of metal type would enable a printer to assemble a series of words, such as a religious text, for printing, and could then be reassembled for another purpose.

Top: Barbara Brownie has used a variety of traditional metal type for her design.

Above: This poster has been created in letterpress by Hand & Eye Letterpress.

Right: Sort, a letterpress printing company,

Here you can see how the metal type has made an indentation in the paper through the pressure applied during the printing process.

*

Everything in the present has been
A D
built on experience from the past, and
R I A
everything in the future is contained in
N F R U
the present. Today's work is anchored
T I G
in the history of human achievement
E R
and, if of value, it becomes a
*
foundation for the future.

This symmetrical letterpress broadside by Christopher Wakeling has a combination of all caps with upper- and lowercase lettering to demonstrate Adrian Frutiger's typeface. The lowercase type is legible as it is intended to be read whereas the uppercase words, in color, are meant to draw attention and cause the viewer to work out the name.

Dan Marino has used an initial letter design in this innovative clock for Downtown Studio.

left: Initial capital letters were often used in medieval manuscripts for decorative purposes and also as markers for the beginning of a section or chapter. This example shows an illustrated capital initial letter used in a music manuscript. Modern-day drop, hanging, or initial caps fulfill similar roles.

below: The design for the Q Yacht website, by Artiva, uses a capital "Q" that resembles a magnifying glass to encourage the reader to focus on the text.

Why is the way we use type important?

When we think of type it is usually in the context of communicating the written word and often, in that process, we don't notice the type itself. We tend to ignore the type or letterforms themselves, as they are usually only a vehicle for the message. This is one of the lessons given to budding typographers: a good or successful typeface is often invisible except to the designer. When you read a newspaper or magazine, unless you are interested in typography, you probably won't notice the typeface that has been used. In fact, if the reader does notice the typeface, or the way it is used, it may be for a negative reason—for example, because it impairs the legibility of the text. This is an issue that we will discuss in chapter 2.

On other occasions type is highly visible, such as when type is used as image, decorative lettering, or calligraphy to enhance the visual appearance of a page and, in this instance, is not the actual message but helps communicate the message. (There are examples, of course, where, either by design or mistake, such type does not help with communication.) An example of a decorative element that enhances communication is the initial or drop capital (cap), which may be highly decorative but also signals a starting point and helps draw the reader's eye to it. This device is commonly used in editorial matter such as novels and magazines.

It is often the person who is using the type, either the designer or the author of the text, who will determine whether the type is to be purely functional or whether it needs enhancement of some sort. When deciding on a typeface or its use, your experience and "eye" in typography will be important. There are many rules and lots of advice available, but you will develop confidence in your own judgment and develop your own style and approach to using type.

Activity

Take an article from a magazine, newspaper, or website and decide where an initial cap would be appropriate. Design an eye-catching initial cap that fits with the theme of the article, the likely readership, and the typeface used.

In this editorial design, Steven Acres of studioimbrue has used a decorative initial cap to draw the reader to the beginning of the text.

Who uses type?

There are probably very few people who don't use type so it would be almost impossible to list everyone who does but, as a starter, they can be roughly categorized as: visual communicators, such as designers, illustrators, and Web developers; writers and educators, such as journalists, authors, and teachers; and information providers, such as scientists, nutritionists, and health professionals. Within each grouping there is a range of business activities that involve the use of type. For example, within the fields of design, illustration, and Web development we will find games designers, packaging designers, video and film makers, textile designers, product designers, signwriters, and calligraphers.

Such people may use type for a variety of purposes, including persuasion, information, illustration, propaganda, instruction, and even decoration. Often these purposes will overlap: for example, a website that provides information may also use decoration and/or illustration to attract the audience.

Choice of typeface and the way it is produced need to be considered in relation to the purpose of the communication. For example, if you were designing a brochure for a legal or accountancy firm, you would normally choose a typeface that conveyed a feeling of reliability and promoted confidence and that did not give the appearance of trying too hard to sell the organization. On the other hand, an advertisement for a festival would be expected to contain more overtly persuasive elements, and the typeface used would reflect this.

Damien Poulain draws attention to this storefront with his use of simple but dramatic red type.

This wine label for the Reggina Estate has been created with calligraphy by Jordan Jelev.

left: Palette Industries use type in an innovative way on this lampshade. The appearance of the letterforms will change when the lamp is lit, and it will project shadow letterforms onto surrounding surfaces.

below: This First World War poster could be interpreted both as propaganda (portraying the enemy as a mad brute), and as persuasion (asking people to enlist). The typeface, and the way it surrounds the image, is typical of billboards and publications of the period.

The restaurant sign (above) uses type for information and promotion whereas the street sign (below) is for information only.

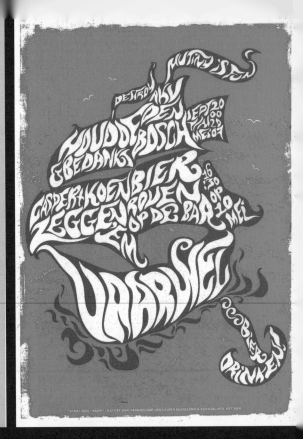

This artwork by Jamie Portch shows the use of type for decorative effect. It accompanies a *New Scientist* article about a new form of terrorist attack using electromagnetic pulses to disable an airplane's electronics systems. The letter "U" has been used in an image that references dropping bombs and magnets.

Attak's distinctive use of hand-rendered type gives a lively and energetic look to this poster.

In this website for the British Heart Foundation, letterforms and words have been used decoratively to make up the heart shape. As you move the cursor over the heart, different headings are highlighted, which,

when clicked, take you to the corresponding areas of the website. In this example, "food4thought" was scrolled over and clicked, which led to the heart shape breaking up and taking the viewer to the section about diet.

Choose any word you like (longer words will give you more letterforms to work with). Produce the word in two different ways, choosing typefaces or letterforms that are suitable for two different contexts: for example, a poster advertising a classical concert and another one advertising a circus.

3. AKADEMIEKONZERT

LUDWIG VAN BEETHOVEN
»Der General« für Orchester, mit Sopran, Chor und Erzähler
»Egmont« op. 84 Text Paul Griffiths
Symphonie Nr. 5 c-Moll op. 67

Leitung Kent Nagano
Sopran Aga Mikolaj
Erzähler Nikolaus Bachler
Chor der Bayerischen Staatsoper

Nationaltheater
26. und 27. Januar, 20.00 Uhr

Bayerisches
Staatsorchester

op: Petar Pavlov constructs 3-dimensional letterforms to look like a tube of chocolates, using color and form to reinforce the word.

above: Frost Design use the transparent quality of glass to good effect in this signage.

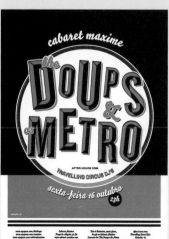

above: Fons Hickmann m23 use a serif typeface for the main heading in this poster—an appropriately restrained choice for a classical-music concert advertisement.

left: Eurico Sá Fernandes has chosen a display typeface to reflect the lively nature of a circus performance at a Lisbon night spot.

GRAFIK: LUDOVIC BALLAND, SIMON PALMIERI
THE REKONBTONS/BASEL

ARNI&IEBDRUCK

RADIO X 94.5

WWW.DASSCHIFF.CH

Where and when is type used?

Type is used in almost all aspects of our daily lives. The list is constantly expanding as new uses, such as texting and smartphone apps, are developing at a rapid pace. These uses may be print-based (posters, leaflets, tickets, signage, board games, books, packaging, maps, instruction manuals, etc.) or screen-based (movie titles, websites, TV ads, computer games, cell phones, tablet computers, digital books, magazines and newspapers, etc.).

Context will influence the way that type is used. In the printed poster on the left, the way type has been applied would not transfer well into a website design, partly because of the portrait format of the poster but also because the capital letters would be more difficult to read on screen than on a billboard. However, it could work as an incrementally developing screen where the words fade in, giving the reader time to absorb them gradually. On the other hand, the series of website screenshots opposite exploit the possibilities inherent in this medium.

In this poster for a music festival, Ludovic Balland mainly uses type to communicate the message, but he also includes a strong frame to delineate the three days of the festival.

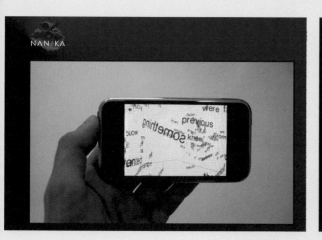

Nanika have used animated type on the
iPhone platform.

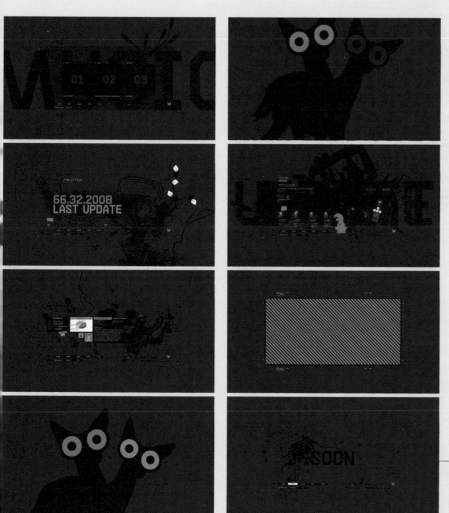

In this series of screenshots from
Comandeer's entertaining website, type and
image have been used to provide a dynamic,
nonlinear entry to the site.

This strong design has been produced in letterpress by Sebastien Carter of the Rampant Lions Press.

Chapter 1 : The basics

This chapter looks at fundamental principles related to the use of type and identifies the terminology used. We will consider the different categories of typeface, such as serif and sans serif, and the main differences between them. Alongside this, we will examine families of type, which include styles such as bold and italic, the structure of letterforms, and how these properties may be used in an experimental and adventurous way both for print and screen.

The anatomy of type

When we talk about a set of letterforms of a particular
design, we refer to it as a typeface or, as it has become a
term in everyday use, a font. Each letterform consists of
one or more of the following parts: serif, ascender,
descender, counter, bar, and stem.

counter

ascender

bar

stem

serif

descender

This diagram shows the essential parts of a
letterform referred to in this book. Further
diagrams focusing on individual components
will be included later in the chapter.

Categories of type

Typefaces may be divided into two main categories: serif and sans serif. The difference between these is basically that serif typefaces are based on Roman incised lettering, which features small strokes at the ends of letterforms, as seen in the diagram opposite. Sans serif letterforms do not have these strokes—hence "sans," which means "without."

Variations

There are many other sorts of letterform, most of which sit within these broad categories. Examples include block, or slab, serif (which has a large slab rather than a stroke at the ends of the letterform), headline, and script typefaces.

Headline, or display, typefaces are usually intended to draw attention to isolated words, phrases, or short sentences. Such typefaces tend to be eye-catching and attractive but would prove difficult to read in a large block because they often incorporate complex or quirky designs. Display faces may be hand drawn from scratch or be hand- or digitally manipulated variants of an existing typeface. Such typefaces are often available from websites as free downloads. A word of caution: you usually get what you pay for, but there is some excellent experimental work out there—for example, HVD Fonts' Square Pants typeface (see next page).

above: This website by Venture 3/CHI & Partners shows the classic serif typeface designed specifically for *The Times* newspaper and called Times New Roman. You can clearly see the small strokes that form the serifs.

right: A sans serif typeface has been used by Artiva for their logotype at the head of this website page and also in the print example displayed on the website.

left: This playful identity by Doink uses a typeface with a prominent serif. The serifs provide a foundation for the uprights that make the letter A look as if it is standing up, with the button balanced halfway down to form the crossbar.

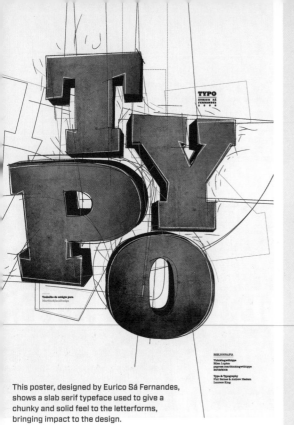

This poster, designed by Eurico Sá Fernandes, shows a slab serif typeface used to give a chunky and solid feel to the letterforms, bringing impact to the design.

Pitfall: It is a common mistake to use a display typeface for sections of text that are meant to be read, such as magazine articles or books. These sections of text are referred to as body type, body text, or copy. We will examine this issue further in the section on legibility (see page 44).

Script typefaces are usually intended to replicate handwriting or calligraphy. As with display or headline typefaces, script typefaces are often difficult to read if used in body text. Because they replicate handwriting, script typefaces work best as a combination of upper and lower case, rather than as all capital letters. You will probably be familiar with one of the most common applications of script typefaces: the invitation card.

top: Atelier Martino&Jaña have used different typefaces to complement each other and the collaged background image, which includes different letterforms.

above: This display typeface, Square Pants by HVD Fonts, is quirky and attracts attention.

clockwise from top left: Insane have used a headline/display typeface in this logotype. The typeface draws on the structure of early hand-drawn letterforms like those produced by monks for medieval manuscripts. Although the typeface is well designed, it is not appropriate for continuous reading as it is quite complex and some of the letterforms do not form instantly recognizable letter shapes.

These hand-constructed letterforms by Eva Blanes illustrate how effective such typefaces can be when used selectively, such as for a single word. But imagine trying to read a paragraph or whole page in this ...

Alejandro Paul's typeface Compendium complements the sophisticated feel of the photograph and text.

Distinctive headline type has been used by Pablo Abad for the heading on this double-page spread.

Ross Elliott has used a script typeface in a bright color on a gray background to produce an attention-grabbing introductory page for his website.

In this poster design Dimitris Kanellopoulos has juxtaposed two different sans serif typefaces to good effect.

Combining typefaces

Many typographic designs call for a combination of typefaces. The way in which different typefaces are used together can have a considerable bearing on the message they communicate and can also affect legibility. For example, you might set the main text on a menu card for a chic bistro in a sans serif typeface to help communicate a modern, pared-down theme, but this effect would be nullified if the titles were set in an elaborate script typeface. Also, combining two display faces may halve rather than double their impact: the typefaces may end up competing for attention and cancel each other out.

However, typeface combination can work very well. Designers will often use contrasting typefaces to show the difference between pieces of information or to emphasize an item. An example of this could be a poster where the name of the event is in one typeface and information such as venue, times, and dates is in another typeface. It is a commonly held principle that two typefaces from the same category, such as sans serifs, do not work well together because they can look too similar. However, as with most rules, there are exceptions. There are a large variety of typefaces that have strong individual characteristics and these may work together.

You will find many examples of combinations of headline or script typefaces used as titles. A headline or script typeface is often used for titles and other short sections. This is in order to differentiate between the sections of information and/or to highlight the importance of the title. Serif and sans serif typefaces lend themselves to body text as they are easier to read.

Some typefaces have a variety of uses (serif fonts tend to be among the most versatile), but some, such as scripts and headline/display faces, have more limited applications—you wouldn't set a novel in a script typeface as it would make it extremely difficult to read.

As you become familiar with the different typefaces, you will find ones that you consider work well together. This is all part of developing your own style.

Activity

Find an example of each of the following categories of typeface in use in both print and screen: serif, sans serif, slab serif, script, display. When you have found examples, experiment with making up words using individual letterforms from the different typefaces to see how they do, or don't, go together.

These are some examples of different sorts of typeface used in print and screen design. Kelsey Allen has used a serif typeface in this quirky design (far right), whereas the sans serif on the Submariners website (right) gives a straightforward feel. The two print designs above contrast a poster for an exhibition about a Catalan novelist, for which Astrid Stavro has chosen a serif typeface (above right), with Ragnar Freyr's poster for a breakbeat concert (above left), which deploys a sans serif typeface for a more modern feel.

Morla has captured the esse of numerous clients, but sho the most extensive opportu with furniture retailer Desi Within Reach, for whom sh served as chief creative and keting officer from 2006 until 2008 (she started ative director in 2005). The position allowed he more fully express the brand's spirit and identit she accomplished through revamping the form

Selecting typefaces

There are a range of considerations when selecting a typeface. These include the genre of text it is to be used for, whether it is to be used on its own or combined with others, what size it will be, whether it is for body text or headlines, whether it is to appear in print or on screen, and what "personality" it needs to convey (see page 31). Lastly, the designer's personal preference should not be overlooked.

When choosing a typeface for body type, it is often useful to have a range of tried-and-true typefaces to draw on. These may be types that you have experimented with yourself or they could be ones you have seen in magazines, books, etc. Some publishers are helpful enough to include on the imprint page the name of the typeface used in the book. The reason behind having a group of typefaces you are familiar with is that you will be accustomed to how they work in a variety of settings, taking into account such factors as size, column measure, and type of paper to be printed on (see chapter 7).

The choice of typeface will also depend on the alphabet that is used. Most typefaces for European alphabets use letterforms based on Roman characters, but these would be unsuitable for other alphabets such as Russian (Cyrillic) or Japanese, because the letterforms are different and the text may also be read in a different direction, such as from right to left or from top to bottom. Braille, which uses texture to communicate the message, is different again. It is interesting to see two or more quite different alphabets used together, as in many webpages, which demonstrate this point. The different features of different alphabets provide creative and experimental opportunities that are facilitated by technological advances.

A variety of sections of body text, including serif and sans serif typefaces at different sizes and settings, have been collected in this scrapbook.

TIP

Keep a scrapbook for examples of good use of particular typefaces in various situations for future reference. These could be your own experiments or work, or cutouts or photocopies from a variety of editorial matter such as newspapers and magazines. Rather than printing out screen- or Web-based work, create a folder of screenshots or use bookmarks.

Amerili Ghasemi has combined two
languages to produce this innovative
design. The Arabic and Roman
letterforms complement each other
and form shapes that work with
the image.

In this brochure HVD Fonts show the family range for the typeface Opal Pro together with some examples of the special characters available and the typeface in use.

Families of type

Some typefaces have been designed with a range of
variations on the basic or standard design. These are
referred to as families and can incorporate a variety of
different styles, such as bold, italic, wide, condensed,
light, outline, etc. Such typefaces are intended to give the
designer the opportunity to combine variants of a typeface
that work well together.

> **(!)** **Pitfall:** When we talk about typeface families,
> we are referring to typefaces that have been
> designed in these formats. This is not to be
> confused with the facility, on most software
> programs, to select an area of type and click a
> button to change its style to, for example,
> italic. Try producing a word using an italic or
> bold typeface and compare this with the same
> word produced in a regular typeface that has
> been italicized using software. It is even
> possible to use the italic button to further
> italicize an italic typeface—the same applies
> to bold versions. Such facilities, however, can
> be useful as a last resort when there is no
> italic or bold version of a typeface available.

Families of typefaces can be particularly useful when you
want to show the difference between two sections of text in
a subtle manner rather than using a completely different
typeface. Many examples of this use of typeface families
can be found in book indexes and dictionaries.

Type families are designed in sets to complement each
other. Families are not always constrained to bold, italic,
etc. Some typefaces have serif and sans serif subfamilies,
which have been designed to work well in conjunction
with each other. Examples include Stone and Rotis.

Ba 🚶
Design & Exploration

*"We shall not cease from exploration and
at the end of our exploring will be to arrive
where we started and know the place for
the first time."*

T. S. Eliot

Websites
Online Presence

Kris D'Amico	Healthways	Cumberland Transit
Foster Mobley	Back Yard Burgers	Exxon Mobil
The Iron Gate	Esoteric Sports	Brite Revolution

Identity
Logo / Branding

Brite Revolution	Foster Mobley	Doorpost Film
Music City Jazz	Greener Solutions	F.M. Allen
Brookside Resort	Digital Nashville	Nashville Music City

Elements & Principles®

Blake Allen's website uses a sans serif
family of type to differentiate between
sections of information.

Expert sets

Another variation that comes under the umbrella of typeface families is the expert set, an extended set of characters required for various specialist purposes. These include, for example: ligatures for joining certain neighboring letterforms; foreign-language glyphs such as German umlauts and French cedillas; and small caps, which are exactly as described—smaller capital letterforms that are designed specifically rather than just reduced in size. Small caps may be used in sections of text that contain acronyms to make them less prominent— if they are in full caps they tend to stand out from the rest of the text. Not all typefaces have expert sets, as each supplementary character has to be designed individually.

This promotion for Wete's free typeface, Deibi, shows the range of glyphs and ligatures available.

Johan Skybäck demonstrates some of the ligatures and small caps available in the expert set of his typeface Södermalm.

HORNSGATAN

Ganska kyligt (BARA 24 GRADER).

DET BLIR FEM KRONOR OCH ARTON ÖRE TACK.

Vad gäspar snäckan?

INTE EN SUSNING KISEN.

15.26 – 17.40

Äppelträd & dödsångest, parkbänkar & ölburkar.

GÖTGATSBACKEN

176 stencoola snubbar.

HUR ERU FUNTAD EGENTLIGEN?!

MEDBORGARPLATSEN

Taxichafförer, de röker som borstbindare allihopa!

SUBORDINATIONSBROTT

To understand the different ways of using members of a typeface family to emphasize a section of text or just one word, choose a short text or poem that has meaning for you. Set this in a typeface that you consider appropriate (it needs to be a typeface that has a good range of family members, such as in the example below). Select words that you think need emphasis and put each of these words into one of the family members of your typeface—for example, light/bold/wide/italic.

There is no *fire* like ***passion***,
There is no ***shark*** like **hatred**,
There is no *snare* like folly,
There is no ***torrent*** like good.

BUDDHA

Members of the Univers family, from Thin Ultra Condensed to Extra Black Extended Oblique, have been used to create emphasis in this Buddhist quotation.

Font | PlayA | 2005

abcdefghijklmnopqrstuvwxyzäöü
ABCDEFGHIJKLMNOPQRSTUVWXYZÄÖÜ
1234567890 (.,;'""'"!?)

Wenn ich König wär, dann würd ich machen, dass die Kinder
morgens in goldenen Kutschen, die von ganz grossen
Hühnern gezogen werden, in der Schule fahren. Die Lehrer
wären Biber wie in dem Comic von dem Schuhgeschäft.
Wenn ich König wär, hätte ich Filzstifte in 10 000 Farben und
könnte gut malen.

Und etwa so gross wie ich?
Und etwa so gross wie ich?
Und etwa so gross wie ich?
Und etwa so gross wie ich?
Und etwa so gross wie ich?
Und etwa so gross wie ich?

Und etwa so gross wie
Und etwa so gross
Und etwa so gr
Und etwa so

Font | SportMonu | Medium | 2004

h
ABCDEFGHIJKLMNOPQRSTUVWXYZÄÖÜ
1234567890 (.,;!?)

WENN ICH KÖNIG WAR, DANN WURD ICH MACHEN, DASS DIE KINDER
MORGENS IN GOLDENEN KUTSCHEN, DIE VON GANZ GROSSEN
HUHNERN GEZOGEN WERDEN, IN DER SCHULE FAHREN. DIE LEHRER
WAREN BIBER WIE IN DEM COMIC VON DEM SCHUHGESCHAFT.
WENN ICH KÖNIG WAR, HATTE ICH FILZSTIFTE IN 10 000 FARBEN
UND KÖNNTE GUT MALEN.

UND ETWA SO GROSS WIE ICH?
UND ETWA SO GROSS WIE ICH?
UND ETWA SO GROSS WIE ICH?
UND ETWA SO GROSS WIE ICH?
UND ETWA SO GROSS WIE ICH?
UND ETWA SO GROSS WIE ICH?

UND ETWA SO GROSS W
UND ETWA SO GRO
UND ETWA SO G
UND ETWA S

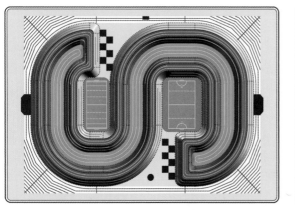

These designs by Martin Woodtli demonstrate
one of his typefaces in different point sizes,
both upper and lower case, as well as its
application within a design where the different
sizes have been used to create hierarchy as
well as interest.

Measurement of type

When discussing specifications with printers, Web developers, or clients, it is useful to be able to communicate exactly what size type you want and, when working on a design, you need to know what type sizes look like in order to select the one you want.

It is difficult to give an accurate method for measuring an individual letterform in a specific typeface and, although there are various measurement units for type in different countries, the point measurement that is used in software packages today has become universal. Point measurements derive from the height of the metal block that the letterforms were originally cast on rather than from the height of the letterforms themselves. You cannot say that because a capital letter "A" of a typeface is 12 points that it measures, for example, 1/8 inch (4 mm) from the base of the type to the top. This measurement is defined by other factors such as the height of ascenders, appearing size, etc.

For guidance, 72 points is equivalent to 1 inch (25.4 mm). In the same way that imperial units (yards, feet, inches) developed over time, relating to such physical measurements as the length of an average human foot and the distance from your nose to the tip of your middle finger (a yard), type measurements mainly relate to the physical use of metal type developed by Gutenberg. Metric measurements have replaced many of these methods of measurement, but the terminology is often still in use and may be used simultaneously. For example, type size is referred to in points, but other measurements are often referred to in millimeters.

Varied sizes of type may be used to create different effects, such as to define the hierarchy of headings, emphasize key sections of text, or indicate a lively layout. An everyday example of hierarchy in action is the magazine article, where the title is usually the most important item and therefore in the largest point size. Pull quotes, intended to draw your attention to the article, need to be emphasized in order to be effective. This continues throughout the layout, so subheadings (crossheads) will be smaller than the title but larger than the body text and so on.

It is useful to understand how some typefaces can look larger or smaller than others even though they are the same point size. This is related to the design of different typefaces and the ratio of the various parts of the letterforms.

As illustrated in this enlarged diagram, point size relates to the metal body that type was originally produced on rather than to the letterform itself.

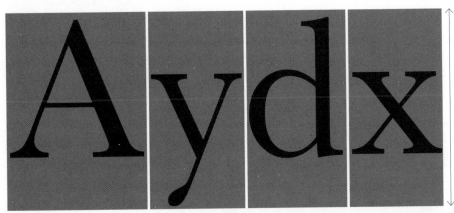

Point size
72 point (1 inch)
Gray areas represent
the metal body

Activity

There are many creative possibilities in using different point sizes, such as pattern and repetition. Draw a wavy line across the width of a letter-size page. Pick a typeface and try to follow the line using the same letterform at different sizes, as in the example shown right, which uses Baskerville Old Face to follow the shape of the line.

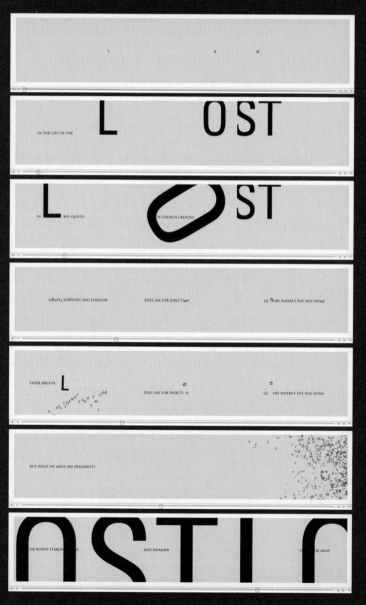

This visual poem, "Lost," has been designed by Re°Nascent to be exhibited across three plasma screens. The animation relies on the juxtaposition and combinations of different sizes of type to attract the audience and communicate the meaning of the poem.

Structure of a letterform

The way a letterform is structured will affect how it works both on its own and combined with other typefaces. It is useful to understand the differences in structure as this helps with identification—it is often difficult to tell one typeface from another if they are similar in style or from the same period.

Franklin Gothicx xGaramond

This diagram demonstrates how different in size two different typefaces can appear at the same point size. The factor that makes the difference is known as the x-height, the height of a lowercase "x" in each typeface.

Q Where would it be useful to have typefaces with different x-heights?

A The typeface used for the question, above, is Century Gothic which has a large x-height. In contrast, the answer is set in Twentieth Century, a typeface with a small x-height. This is an extreme example of the use of contrasting x-heights.

This question-and-answer text is an extreme example of the use of contrast in x-height.

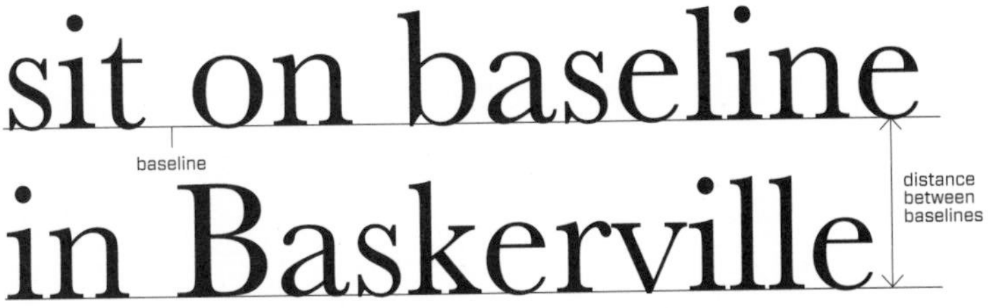

sit on baseline
baseline
in Baskerville
distance
between
baselines

Lines of type sit on a baseline. The distance between two neighboring lines of text is defined as the distance between their respective baselines.

As shown in the diagram above, the x-height is the distance from the top of a lowercase "x" to its base. This may vary depending on the design of the typeface: for example, Century Gothic has a large x-height whereas Twentieth Century has a small x-height. This is often referred to as the appearing size of a typeface because it affects how it appears in print or on screen—a letterform with a large x-height will usually look larger at the same point size than one with a smaller x-height. A good way of seeing the difference x-height can make is to print a page of type in two columns and use a typeface with a small x-height in the first column and one with a large x-height in the second. As with other combinations of letterforms/typefaces, this difference may be used to advantage when designing, for example, a question-and-answer section of a magazine where you wish to differentiate between two voices, as in the example left.

The x-height relates to the baseline of a section of type: this is the invisible line that the type sits on. The baseline is important as it is used to define the distance between two lines of text, which is referred to as linespacing or leading (pronounced "ledding"). This distance may be increased or decreased depending on the typeface and the effect you are trying to achieve. This issue is covered in more depth in chapter 2.

It is worth noting that letterforms that have a rounded base, such as "s" or "a," do not sit exactly on the baseline but curve slightly below it. The reason for this is that if they did sit exactly on the baseline, they would appear to be higher than the rest of the text. Try it out and see for

yourself. This highlights the need to use your experience and "eye" in typography, rather than relying on measurements alone.

In this design by Untitled, the yellow rule underneath the baseline highlights the way that rounded letterforms drop slightly below this line whereas flat ones sit exactly on it.

! **Pitfall:** Printed type, and often that on screen, may be much smaller than you think. When we are typing letters, the default size for most programs is 12 point, but if this were used as body text in magazines, books, or websites, it would look too big. This relates to the appearing size mentioned before. Many publications use type as small as 8.5 point and yet this does not necessarily look small to the reader.

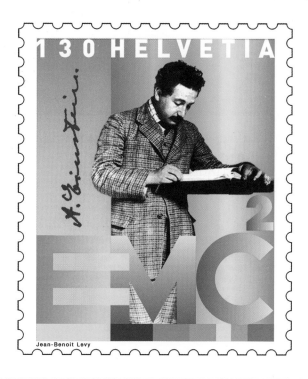

Jean-Benoit Levy

Counterforms

You will have seen in the diagram at the beginning of this chapter (see page 22) that one of the essential parts of a letterform is known as a counter. A counter, or counterform, is the part left behind by the shape of the letterform—such as the space within the letter "O." This is often referred to as negative space. Counterforms can be used to good effect when designing. For example, the counterforms of the letter "B" may be filled with a different color to form positive shapes. Counterforms do not necessarily have to be totally enclosed: for example, the partially open space inside the letter "U" is still a counterform.

In this design for a postage stamp, Jean-Benoît Lévy has emphasized the counterforms in the letter "E" of the E=mc² equation, blending them with the equals sign for further impact.

This humorous response, by KO:KE, to a call for designs on the letter "B" by the branding and design agency Bunch has the yolks of two fried eggs as counterforms.

"Theater and Engineering" exhibition publicity
by Martin Woodtli, Switzerland

The design was in response to a brief for publicity material for an exhibition, organized in 2008 by the MIT List Visual Arts Center, illustrating the 1966 "9 Evenings: Theater and Engineering" events in New York. These included experiments combining diverse genres such as music, theater, dance, film, and video, and put the prominent artists involved—including John Cage, Deborah Hay, Steve Paxton, Robert Rauschenberg, and David Tudor—in contact with experienced engineers. Initiated by Billy Klüver from Bell Telephone Laboratories,

it was hoped that this interdisciplinary collaboration would lead to specially designed equipment.

Martin's work attempts to convey the relationship between art and technology that the exhibition promoted. He used typefaces that reflected the feel of 1960s and '70s New York and created new typeface forms to suggest three-dimensional neon signage. The white type stands out from the strong colors of the imagery and background.

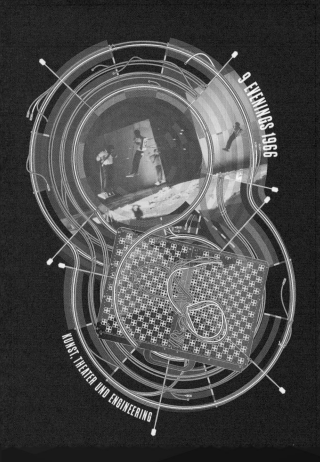

9 EVENINGS 1966: KUNST, THEATER UND ENGINEERING
MUSEUM FÜR GESTALTUNG ZÜRICH
30. JULI BIS 7. SEPTEMBER 2008

New York, Oktober 1966: Neun spektakuläre Abende in der 69th Regiment Armory Hall verbinden Musik, Theater, Tanz, Film und Video und markieren die Geburtsstunde der interaktiven Performance. Erstmals begegneten sich dabei versierte Ingenieure und profilierte Kunstschaffende in einem kreativen Prozess. Billy Klüver von den Bell Telephone Laboratories hatte John Cage, Lucinda Childs, Öyvind Fahlström, Alex Hay, Deborah Hay, Steve Paxton, Yvonne Rainer, Robert Rauschenberg, David Tudor und Robert Whitman für dieses interdisziplinäre Experiment begeistern können. Die vom MIT List Visual Arts Center produzierte Ausstellung veranschaulicht die Verbindung von Elektronik und Live-Aufführung vor grossem Publikum und damit auch deren aktuell gebliebene Haltung gegenseitiger Neugier von Kunst und Technik.

VERNISSAGE: Dienstag, 29. Juli, 19 Uhr
Es sprechen:
Giaco Schiesser, Direktor Departement Kunst & Medien, Zürcher Hochschule der Künste ZHdK
Andres Janser, Kurator Museum für Gestaltung Zürich
Catherine Morris, Kuratorin der Ausstellung, New York

KONZERT: Samstag / Sonntag, 6. / 7. September, 20 – 01 Uhr
Zwei Ensembles der ZHdK spielen ständlich an der Langen Nacht der Museen:
John Cage, «Variations I – III» und «Variations IV – VI» (1958 – 66)

FÜHRUNGEN
— Sonntag, 3. August, 15 Uhr
Susanne Hillman, Kunsthistorikerin, Zürich
— Dienstag, 5. August, 18.30 Uhr
Nils Röller, Dozent Vertiefung Mediale Künste, ZHdK
— Dienstag, 12. August, 18.30 Uhr
Cynthia Gavranic, Kuratorin Museum für Gestaltung Zürich
— Dienstag, 19. August, 18.30 Uhr
Tina Mantel, Dozentin Tanz, ZHdK
— Dienstag, 26. August, 18.30 Uhr
Barbara Liebster, Dozentin Szenografie, ZHdK
— Dienstag, 2. September, 18.30 Uhr
Bruno Karrer, Dozent Departement Musik, ZHdK
— Sonntag, 7. September, 15 Uhr
Andres Janser, Kurator Museum für Gestaltung Zürich
— Spezialführungen (auch in Englisch) auf Anfrage:
T: +41 (0)43 446 67 10 oder marilena.cipriano@zhdk.ch

ÖFFNUNGSZEITEN
• Dienstag – Donnerstag 10 – 20 Uhr, Freitag – Sonntag 10 – 17 Uhr • Bundesfeiertag 1. August 10 – 17 Uhr
• Lange Nacht der Museen 6. / 7. September 19 – 02 Uhr • Montags geschlossen

MUSEUM FÜR GESTALTUNG ZÜRICH
• Ausstellungsstrasse 60, CH-8005 Zürich • Tel +41 (0)43 446 67 67, www.museum-gestaltung.ch
• Tram 4 und 13, Haltestelle Museum für Gestaltung

Design: Martin Woodtli — Photo: Peter Moore © Estate of Peter Moore / VAGA, NYC — Zürcher Hochschule der Künste, Zürcher Fachhochschule

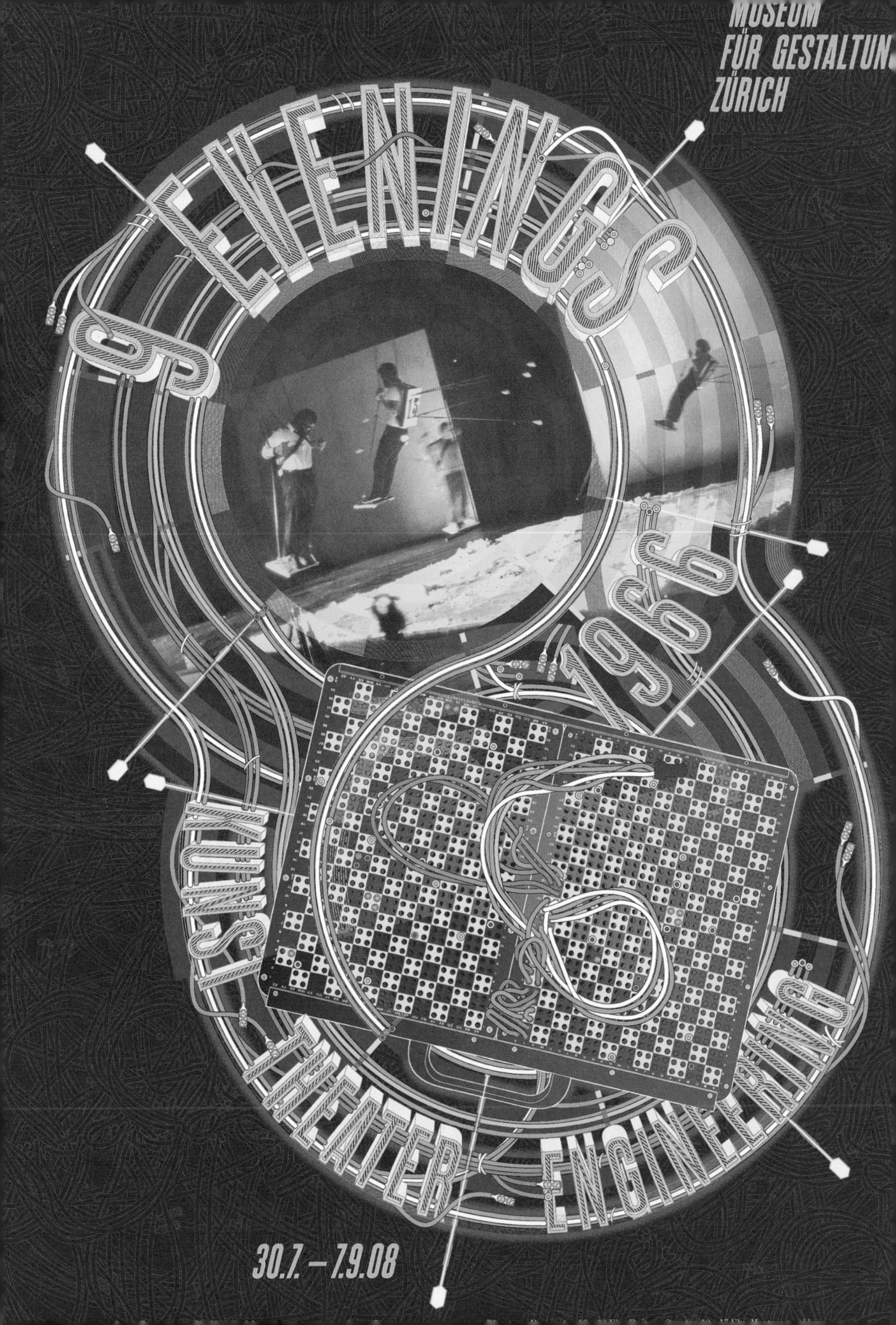

SEVENINGS

MUSEUM FÜR GESTALTUN ZÜRICH

1960

THEATER ENGINEERINGS

30.7. – 7.9.08

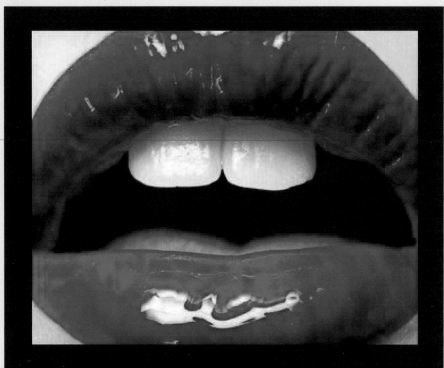

Tens curiositat?
descobreix-la

museu de
l'eròtica

La Rambla, 96 bis
08002 Barcelona
Telf. 93 318 98 65
Fax: 93 301 08 96
info@erotica-museum.com
www.erotica-museum.com

De dilluns a diumenge...
d'Octubre a Maig de 11 a 21 hs.
de Juny a Setembre de 10 a 24 hs.

Eva Blanes uses reversed-out and red type as
contrast, as well as reflection in the image, to
create a striking poster design.

Chapter 2 : Using the typeface

In this chapter we will discuss considerations in using type, such as the choice of typeface, and explore creative approaches to typographic issues. Typefaces will be considered in the light of legibility, readability, their use in layout, and their relationship with any images used. Alongside this, we will introduce type terminology and the use of such devices as ligatures and dashes. These will be supported by successful examples of screen- and print-based work.

Legibility and readability

Type is a means of communicating the written word and therefore legibility and readability are important. Broadly, type is legible if individual letterforms can be readily deciphered; it is readable if it is presented in an accessible and/or engaging way. A shorter line length, for example, is more readable than a longer line length, with 50–80 characters per line, including spaces, thought to be a good column measure.

We've all come across sections of text that have not engaged us even though the content of the text itself may well have been of interest. Used for body text, a dark, heavy typeface may be less legible than a lighter version, because the shapes of the letters are harder to distinguish in a small size compared with regular letterforms.

There are many factors that can affect legibility and readability, such as choice of upper- or lowercase letterforms, length of line, letter and word spacing, size of type, and color or tone of text. We will cover the main issues here.

This design by Renato Forster uses a short line length for the body text to aid readability.

Ludovic Balland has used short line lengths for readability on this engaging poster, where information needs to be communicated quickly and concisely.

You will probably find that this first section of text, produced in Helvetica Neue 6 point on 8 point leading, is more easy to read than the following section of text. This is because, in the first example the line length (measure) is shorter while in the second example there are a large number of words on each line that are difficult to absorb in one go. It is thought that a good column measure for reading is between 50 and 80 characters, including spaces, per line.

This second section will probably be more challenging to read. This is because, in the first example the line length (measure) is shorter while in this example, there are a large number of words on each line. It is difficult to absorb a high number of words across one line in one go. It is thought that a good column measure for reading is between 50 and 80 characters, including spaces, per line.

In this example the first section of text is easily read, whereas the second section is more challenging. The reader finds it more difficult to absorb the larger number of words per line, and may have to reread more often.

The examples here show the same text produced in different ways. The first section has been produced using Gill Sans and the second section uses Gill Sans Ultra Bold. It is clear that the second example might put you off reading as the typeface is dark and heavy.

The examples here show the same text produced in different ways. The first section has been produced using Gill Sans and the second section uses Gill Sans Ultra Bold. It is clear that the second example might put you off reading as the typeface is dark and heavy.

A heavy version of a typeface may affect legibility because the heavier typeface is less easy to decipher in sections of body text than the regular typeface that people are accustomed to reading. In this instance Gill Sans Regular has been used on the left column and Gill Sans Ultra Bold on the right.

Die ·Typographen· waren mit verschiedenartigen Interessen. Und mit unterschiedlichem Niveau und Ausbildungstand. Die erste Aufgabe im vorliegenden Heft wurde ausschließlich von Schülern gelöst, die am Anfang ihres Typographie Unterrichtes standen. Dabei zeigte sich, daß größte Schwierigkeiten beim logischen Gliedern eines Textes auftraten. Diese Erfahrung machte ich mit Klassen der letzten Jahre ebenfalls. Das zeigt, welche komplexe Materie im Fach ·Typographie· vermittelt wird und wie langwierig dieser Prozeß verläuft. Daher drängt sich immer stärker die Frage auf: Wie kann man Typographie innerhalb von zwei Jahren so vermitteln, daß der Schüler selbständig entscheiden lernt, ein gegebenes Manuskript in einen typographischen Entwurf umzusetzen? Erste Voraussetzung dafü scheint mir das Gefühl absoluter Entscheidungsfreiheit zu sein. Freilich eine Freiheit, unter der mehr die Verfügbarkeit der graphischen Möglichkeiten zu verstehen ist. Und Entscheidungen, die aus der Aufgabe und deisen Möglichkeiten abgeleitet werden. Da jede Entscheidung, kann beim Umsetzen eines Textes in Typographie eine Fehlenscheidung sein. Auch das muß der Schüler lernen zu erkennen, um daraus vielleicht einen neuen Ansatzpunkt für seine Arbeit zu gewinnen. Deshalb wird in meinen Unterricht nicht skizziert. Die typographische Realität ist das abgesetzte Wort. Und nur die zeigt seine Länge, sein Verhältnis zu anderen Wörtern, zum gesamten Text un zum ihn umgebenden Raum mit seinin Begrenzungen. Zur Verfügung standen jedem Schüler ein maschinengeschriebenes Manuskript. Unsere Schule kennt keinen unit im Texten. Und auch keine Lehrfächer, in denen Textprobleme behandelt werden. Die Schüler können aus diesem keine selbst konzipierten Texte in die Typographie-Werkstatt mitbringen. Das wäre zum Beispiel deshalb sinnvoll, die solchem Texte zugrunde liegende Konzeption auch für die Konzeption der Typographie verwendet werden kann. s eine susgezeichnete Hilfe für die logische Strukturierung des Textes und für die Bestimmung von Schrift und Satzart äre, Ohne diese Kenntnis der textlichen Konzeption — also ohne Kenntnis der praktischen Aufgabe und geplanten Bede ung eines Textes — bleibt die Typographie auf ihren syntaktischen Möglichkeiten beschränkt. Also: Wenn die semantisch und pragmatischen Funktion eines Textes erkannt und verstanden sind, können die vielfältigen syntaktischen Möglich en sinnvoll eingesetzt werden. Ich betone das deshalb, weil ich mir davon eine entscheidende Objektivierung des Leh prozasses verspreche. Einfacher ausgedrückt: Ein bißchen weniger auf Lehrmeinungen und Gefühlen gegründeten und σ it letztlich für Schüler und Lehrer noch produktiveren Unterricht. Zur Verfügung standen dem Schüler 4 Wochenstund um in der Typographie-Werkstatt zu arbeiten. Für das immer wichtiger werdende Kommunikationsmedium ·Typog sind 4 Wochenstuden anachronistisch. Sie reichen kaum für die Vermittlung handwerklicher Fertigkeiten. nde Druck entstand zwischen November 1970 und März 1971. Daran ist abzulesen, daß ein Viertel der Aufgabe geopfer werden mußte. Night aus ignoranz gegenüber anderen Aufgaben, sondern aus Gründen didaktischer Not. Dann ist weiterhin abzulesen, daß andere dringende Probleme überhaupt nicht behandelt nten· ich denke spielsweise an die Aufarbeitung der verschiedenen typographischen Theorien. An nicht- sogenannte ·technische Typographie·. An komplexe pruchsvoll: Rasterprobleme und typographische Programme im Verla ɘ esen. Die Liste ließe sich belieb ig fortsetzen. Die ·Typographen· waren Schüler mit verschiedenartigen Interessen. Und mit unterschiedlichem Niveau und Ausbildungsstand. Die erste Aufgabe im vorliegenden Heft wurde aussch lich von Schülern gelöst, die am Anfang ihres Typographie Unterrichtes standen. Dabei zeigte sich, daß größte Schwierigkeiten beim logischen Gliedern eines Textes auftraten. Diese Erfahrung machte mit Klassen der letzten re ebenfalls. Das zeigt, welche komplexe Materie im Fach ·Typographie· vermittelt wird une wie langwierig dieser rozeß verläuft. Daher drängt sich immer stärker die Frage auf: Wie kann man Typographie innerhalb von zwei hren so vermitteln, daß der Schüler selbständig entscheiden lernt, ein gegebenes Manuskript in einen typogr schen Entwurf umzusetzen? Erste Voraussetzung dafü scheint mir das Gefühl absoluter Entscheidungsfreiheit sein. Freilich eine Freiheit, unter der mehr die Verfügbarkeit der typographischen Möglichkeiten zu stehen ist. Und Entscheidungen, die aus der Aufgabe und deisen Möglichkeiten abgeleitet werden. Da jede Entsch dung, die weitgehed durch Vorlieben, Unkenntnis und Unverständnis bestimmt wird, die also weitgehend schon zuvor eststeht, kann beim Umsetzen eines Textes in Typographie eine Fehlenscheidung sein. Auch das muß der Schüler lernen erkennen, um daraus vielleicht einen neuen Ansatzpunkt für seine Arbeit zu gewinnen. Deshalb wird in meinen Unterric nicht skizziert. Die typographische Realität ist das abgesetzte Wort. Und nur die zeigt seins Länge, sein Verhältnis zu Wörtern, zum gesamten Text un zum ihn umgebenden Raum mit seinin Begrenzungen. Zur Verfügung

Alex Cornell has experimented creatively with deliberate illegibility and unreadability here. The extreme difficulty of reading this text draws the reader's attention.

Upper and lower case

Care needs to be taken in the setting of text in upper case rather than in the normal mixture of upper- and lowercase letters. You may have noticed, while being immersed in a novel or other large body of text, that you are not consciously reading each letter, word, or even sentence. The same text set in capital letters would require much more concentration to avoid losing the overall meaning of the text. When we read, we read the word shapes that letters combine to form rather than the individual letters: lowercase letterforms have a variety of shapes and profiles whereas capital, or uppercase ones have similar profiles, which makes them more difficult to distinguish between. So, text in all capital letters is often more difficult to read than that in lower case or a combination of upper and lower case.

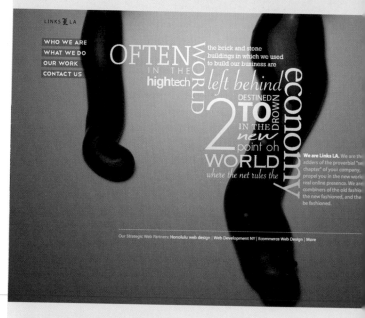

This website by Ravi Vora for Links LA uses all caps combined with upper and lower case for a lively design where a combination of upper and lower case has been used for titles and the main text is in lower case for reading.

design@Typographic have used all caps to create strong moving shapes in this multimedia design. The words are only legible for short periods and are intended to draw attention to the content.

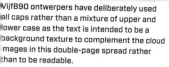

Vijf890 ontwerpers have deliberately used all caps rather than a mixture of upper and lower case as the text is intended to be a background texture to complement the cloud images in this double-page spread rather than to be readable.

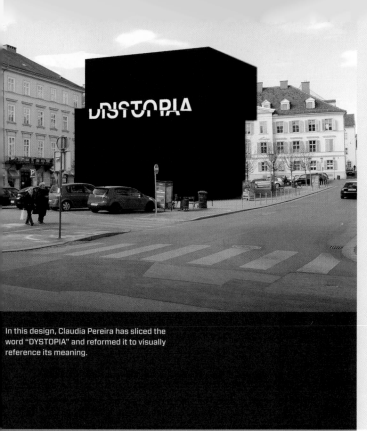

Investigate how much of a letterform needs to be seen for it to be legible. Render the letters "a," "e," "g," "k," and "q" in lower case at a large size, such as 120 point. Experiment with subtracting parts of the letterform until it is no longer recognizable. Try this activity with a serif and sans serif typeface, as in the example below, where Cooper and Century Gothic have been used.

In this design, Claudia Pereira has sliced the word "DYSTOPIA" and reformed it to visually reference its meaning.

In the experiment using Cooper, the letterform is recognizable until the third crop, whereas using Century Gothic the letterform becomes difficult to recognize after the second crop.

left: Artiva have sliced the capital letters and reformed them to make an image for their business card. You will notice that the words are not as easy to read when you do not have the complete letterform.

below: Pentagram have used sections of letterforms in this effective package design for Saks.

On the reverse of this poster, Atelier Martino&Jaña have created a dynamic layout where different leadings have been used to help differentiate between sections of text.

This paragraph is set in 6 point Perpetua with 4 point linespacing. Linespacing can affect the ease with which a section of text may be read. The typeface, its size, and the line length are important factors in selecting linespacing.

This paragraph is set in 6 point Perpetua with 6 point linespacing. Linespacing can affect the ease with which a section of text may be read. The typeface, its size, and the line length are important factors in selecting linespacing.

This paragraph is set in 6 point Perpetua with 9 point linespacing. Linespacing can affect the ease with which a section of text may be read. The typeface, its size, and the line length are important factors in selecting linespacing.

This paragraph is set in 6 point Perpetua with 11 point linespacing. Linespacing can affect the ease with which a section of text may be read. The typeface, its size, and the line length are important factors in selecting linespacing.

This paragraph is set in 6 point Perpetua with 13 point linespacing. Linespacing can affect the ease with which a section of text may be read. The typeface, its size, and the line length are important factors in selecting linespacing.

This paragraph is set in 6 point Perpetua with 18 point linespacing. Linespacing

can affect the ease with which a section of text may be read. The typeface, its

size, and the line length are important factors in selecting linespacing.

above: This demonstrates how decreasing and increasing the spacing between lines of text can affect readability.

below: Tracking can have a marked effect on the legibility of a section of type, whether black on white or white reversed out of black.

The adjustment of space between letterforms in sections of text is called tracking
The adjustment of space between letterforms in sections of text is called tracking
The adjustment of space between letterforms in sections of text is called tracking
The adjustment of space between letterforms in sections of text is called tracking
The adjustment of space between letterforms in sections of text is called tracking
The adjustment of space between letterforms in sections of text is called tracking
The adjustment of space between letterforms in sections of text is called tracking
The adjustment of space between letterforms in sections of text is called tracking
The adjustment of space between letterforms in sections of text is called tracking
The adjustment of space between letterforms in sections of text is called tracking
The adjustment of space between letterforms in sections of text is called tracking
The adjustment of space between letterforms in sections of text is called tracking

Line measure and spacing

As discussed earlier, another issue relating to the way we see text is line measure. We find it difficult to read lines of text over a certain length or number of words because of the way our eyes take in information. You will notice that the majority of books and magazines do not use a long line measure except occasionally in small amounts.

Not only the length of line but also the distance between two lines of text may affect legibility and readability. If, at the end of a line, your eye is not easily drawn to the beginning of the next one, the text may be difficult to read. This can happen if the leading (linespacing) is too great or too small.

Spaces between letters and words

The distance between letters and words is another aspect of spacing that may affect legibility and readability. The adjustment of space between individual letterforms is usually referred to as kerning, and the spacing between letters across a section of text is known as tracking. A good example of the need for kerning is where a capital "A" and "V" are adjacent (see below). If the space between the two letterforms is not decreased, they look too far apart. Tracking may affect the density of a section of text, making it easier or more difficult to read. This is particularly noticeable when you use a light text on a dark background, which is referred to as reversed-out text. Some reversed-out text may be difficult to read unless the designer adds a little more space than normal between characters.

 TIP Most typefaces have automatically kerned pairs, which helps to avoid obvious letterspacing problems.

right: In the top example, the spacing between letterforms has been adjusted, whereas in the bottom example no kerning has been applied.

How would you even out the apparent large space where the "W" follows the "A"? Experiment with different kerning between "A" and "W" in the word "CLAWS" (or a similar word). You can do this using software or by tracing a print of the word.

TIP It helps to work at a high magnification, and you will see the spaces more clearly if you squint at the word or look at it in a mirror.

Kerning and tracking have many creative applications, such as pattern making or logo design. Experiment with forming shapes and patterns by adjusting the tracking on a word.

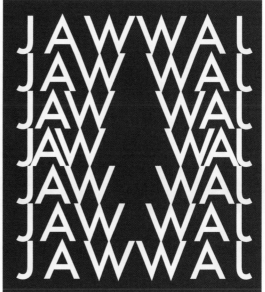

left: The logo for the Victoria & Albert Museum suggests kerning where the ampersand overlaps part of the letter "A" and replaces the bar with kerned space between this and the letter "V."

above: In this example the word "JAW" has been typeset in Futura and then repeated six times with the tracking gradually decreasing and then increasing. The resulting pattern has been duplicated and inverted to form a shape reminiscent of an open jaw.

Andreas Hidber the large
ly overlaying the image, does
e page. In a darker color it

18 | IMAGINE – DAS FESTIVAL GEGEN RASSISMUS – MAGAZINE 2009

FREITAG 12.6.2009   BARFÜSSERBÜHNE

18:00 – 18:45
KNACKEBOUL
19:15 – 19:30
ERÖFFNUNGSREDE, NICO HERZIG
20:00 – 21:30
DAN LE SAC VS. SCROOBIUS PIP (UK)
22:15 – 23:45
KISSOGRAM (DE)

KLOSTERHOFBÜHNE
17:45 – 18:30
JAMES GRUNTZ
19:00 – 19:45
SEPIA
20:30 – 21:30
CASSEROL
22:00 – 23:45
MARYGOLD

KLEINKUNSTBÜHNE
18:45 – 19:15
TUBABU BALAN
19:30 – 19:45
KALASRI
21:30 – 22:00
CHRISTIAN ZIEGLER

SAMSTAG 13.6.2009   BARFÜSSERBÜHNE

14:00 – 14:45
FEET PEALS
15:15 – 15:15
MAD MANOUSH
17:00 – 18:00
GISBERT ZU KNYPHAUSEN (DE)
19:00 – 20:00
HUCK FINN
20:30 – 21:30
MEDALLIST (UK)
22:15 – 23:45
TRIGGERFINGER (BE)

KLOSTERHOFBÜHNE
14:00 – 14:45
LADINA ROBÉRT
15:15 – 16:00
BELA ROLA
16:30 – 17:15
FLINK
17:45 – 18:30
MATTO
19:00 – 20:00
LUCKY JOY
20:30 – 21:30
MON PETIT PONEY
22:00 – 23:45
BALKANEXPRESS

KLEINKUNSTBÜHNE
14:45 – 15:00 & 18:30 – 18:45
LUKAS HILFIKER
15:00 – 17:00
ANIMATION PLAY4YOU
16:15 – 16:45
DIE IMPRONAUTEN
18:15 – 19:30
LAURIN BUSER
20:00 – 20:25
FAMBA MADOKERO

MAGAZINE 2009 | 19

in this example, yellow text
a white background is not
ut, nor is the reversed-out
e text on a yellow background.

Color and size

Using colored type or type on a colored background
can be an effective way of enhancing communication or
attracting attention. Before taking this path, however, it is
worth experimenting with different combinations. Some
color combinations may be too lacking in contrast to be
easily read, particularly at a small size—one example
being yellow on a white background. Some combinations
of colors may cause problems, such as putting two
complementary colors together—for example, green
and red. This causes a visual disturbance where the two
colors touch and therefore makes reading difficult. There
are technical issues relating to use of color in print, such
as how the colors fit together, which we will cover later
(see page 193).

 Pitfall: Red and green are the two colors most
commonly confused in color blindness, and so
this may be a risky pairing.

A common misconception about legibility of type is that
bigger is better. This is not necessarily the case: the
appropriateness of the size of type is affected by many
factors, such as the line length, the typeface, and the role
the text plays in the layout (for example, whether it is a
title or a section of body text). Although the chosen size
depends on the typeface design and its x-height (see page
37), you rarely find 12-point type used in the body text of
editorial and commercial publications.

The visual vibration between the
complementary colors blue and orange
has been used to dramatic effect in this
cover design by Hackenschuh.com design.

Andrea Bussetti has combined reversed-out
and red type to create contrast on this
notepad and carrier.

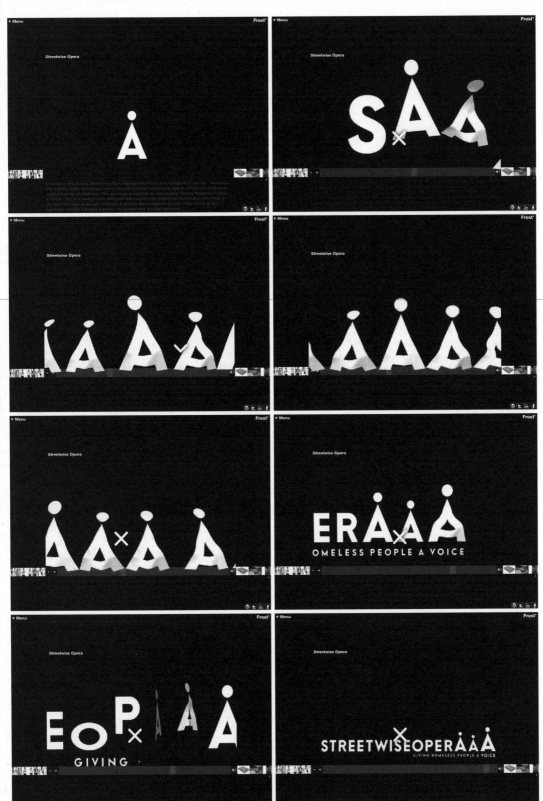

above: This design by Sylvia Aranda demonstrates that type at a small point size can be legible and readable.

right: The series of webpages for Wood restaurant and bar uses a small point size for the body text, which still remains legible because there is plenty of space between the lines of text.

This webpage shows Artiva's use of a
sans serif typeface to produce a simple,
easy-to-read design.

The typeface

The choice of the typeface itself is an obvious but often
overlooked factor in legibility and readability. The suitability
of a typeface for a specific text is subject to a range of
factors, such as whether it is used for print or screen. Some
type designers believe that for large chunks of text such as
a novel, a serif typeface is easier to read than a sans serif
because the serifs help lead the eye across the words.
For type on screen the opposite is said to be true, mainly
because of screen resolution and the fact that screens are
never really static. Other designers don't subscribe to
these fixed views and would rather experiment with a
range of typefaces that suit the content and the context.

Background

While placing text over a background other than a flat color can produce eye-catching results, there are certain considerations to bear in mind. Beware when laying text over an image that contains many variations of tone, because it is likely that some of the tones will be similar to the color of the text. For example, black text becomes difficult to see when it is placed over a dark tonal area. Texture represented in a background image may cause the same sort of problem, because the different patterns can interfere with the letterforms.

Paper stock

The material, usually paper, on which a design is printed is known as the stock. Sometimes the texture of the stock can cause problems with legibility. If the surface has a rough texture, the printed type may not cover the entire area intended: this is more likely to happen if the typeface is fine or has small counterforms (see page 39). This may also be the case when printing on absorbent stock, which may cause the ink to bleed.

Côme de Bouchony overcomes legibility issues in text over image by using a heavy typeface and strong transparent color.

An experiment with the effect created by print on porous paper.

Type on screen

When working on a design for screen, the range of screens that are out there, both in terms of size and quality, may affect legibility and/or readability. The different screen resolutions will change the way the type appears on the screen. For example, a low or poor screen resolution such as 640x480ppi (pixels per inch) will produce a larger but less distinct image than a high resolution such as 1920x1200ppi.

TIP — If you normally work on a screen set at high resolution, check how your design appears at a lower resolution.

When designing for the Web, the appearance size of your design will vary according to the size of the viewer's screen and/or the size of the window/s. It is advisable to work at the minimum size a screen will be viewed at to counteract any problems with legibility. This can result in some type looking larger than intended but at least it should be legible for all users.

Although we have discussed these issues as barriers to legibility and readability, when designing you can use most of them to make something visually exciting. For example, a textured stock that causes parts of letterforms to misprint can create a distressed or handmade quality. Some typefaces, such as Tapeworm (see below), have been designed to appear distressed. Distressing may be simulated for use in screen- or Web-based design to add texture and interest.

This webpage, designed by Lauren Burke, uses simulated misprinted type and image to give a feeling of immediacy. The hand-produced effect also contrasts well with the more controlled digital typeface used in the body text.

Ryan Spacey has used a traditional printing effect to produce this poster. As with Lauren Burke's website design (top), the misprinted letterforms give a sense of immediacy and a bespoke feel to the design.

AÆBCDEFGHIJKLN

Tapeworm Regular, designed by Lloyd Springer of TypeArt Foundry Inc., simulates the effect created when letterpress is either under-inked or has insufficient pressure applied in press.

Activity

Design a poster either for screen or for print that incorporates hand-carved and printed letterforms together with digital printing, as shown here. In our example, the student has carved a letterform into half a raw potato and then used thick acrylic paint as the ink. The letterform has been overprinted on a section of body text produced on an ordinary desktop printer. When the paint was dry, the entire image was scanned so that it could be viewed on screen. Using a potato print is a fun and easy way of producing this effect and also provides plenty of opportunity to experiment with shape, color, and texture (you don't have to use a potato—lots of other root vegetables, such as turnips, are just as easy to use). Please remember to take care when using sharp instruments.

In the first stage of this exercise the student identifies a section of a nursery rhyme and produces a typographic design in Garamond using a design software program, then prints it out on an inkjet printer.

Next she assembles her tools. They include a pen to draw the shape, a sharp kitchen knife and craft knife to carve it out, acrylic paint, a brush, a cutting board to work on, a small piece of cardboard to squeeze the paint onto, and, of course, half a potato.

Having incised around the outline of the letterform and the counters with the craft knife, the student uses a kitchen knife to cut away the large nonprinting areas of potato from around the letterform and to dig out the counters. She then goes round the shape again with a craft knife to tidy up the edges.

With carving now complete, the student brushes paint onto the small piece of card and dips the letterform into it ready for printing.

The letterform is printed for the first time.

The student is trying to echo the fading out of the letter "g" on the inkjet print by repeatedly printing without re-inking the potato.

She experiments on several printouts of the nursery rhyme before deciding on a final design.

This double-page spread by Atelier Martino&Jaña makes use of the contrast between justified, ranged-left, and centered text to give variety.

Ranged-right text is commonly used for languages that read right to left, such as Hebrew—as in this double-page spread by Dan Alexander & Co.

Paragraphs

As we discussed earlier in this chapter, leading, kerning, and tracking can affect how type performs on a page. There are other factors relating to paragraphs or sections of body text that may have an impact on legibility and/or readability. Such factors can determine how the type looks and therefore how it is interpreted. One of the most important is paragraph alignment: whether text is aligned (or ranged) left or right, justified, or centered. The most commonly used alignments in Western design are left aligned (also referred to as ragged right because of the way the right-hand line endings do not align with the column edge) and justified. Justified text is spread across the column measure so that it aligns with both sides of the column. Right alignment (ragged left—the opposite of left aligned) and centering are less frequently used in body text, for reasons of readability. The eye finds it difficult to cope with the fact that in each of these two alignments the starting points of lines of text are not aligned vertically.

There are many examples where different alignments are combined to create emphasis and visual effect. One is in movie titles where right- and left-aligned text are butted up against each other to differentiate between two sections of information (for example, role and actor) and give a mirrored effect.

There are some who hold the view that justified text can never be justified. Because the spacings between words can be quite wide in justified text, it takes a lot of skill and experience (or just plain luck) to ensure that a block of text does not contain "rivers." Rivers are formed when a series of large gaps between words link together into a trickle-like pattern down the page. They can be visually distracting and therefore affect readability, particularly for those with dyslexia or visual impairments and, in our view, look ugly anyway unless designed for a specific effect as in the example shown on page 60. Rivers can be seen more clearly if you squint at text, hold it upside down, or view it in a mirror.

Justified text throws up a decision relating to hyphenation of words at the ends of lines. It is generally considered that hyphenation is a bad thing, mainly because it can cause visual disturbance and it looks ugly. However, it may be a necessary evil to achieve the visual uniformity that is the

These webpage designs by Staynice use a variety of text alignments to aid navigation and differentiate between categories of content.

"PROFESSIONALIZE YOUR DESIGN-SKILLS, ENHANCE YOUR KNOWLEDGE IN THE USE OF NEW TECHNOLOGIES, EXPLORE NEW NARRATIVE STRATEGIES, DEVELOP YOUR PERSONAL ENTREPRENEURSHIP, BUILD AN INTERNATIONAL NETWORK." ▶▶

INFORMATION
PROGRAM / EVENTS
APPLICATION
CONTACT
SHOWCASE
ABOUT US
PARTNERS

MASTER ANIMATION
avans hogeschool
akv|st|joost

PROGRAM 2011-2012 NOW OPEN FOR APPLICATION

You are now able to apply to the master Animation program 2011-2012. Selection days are scheduled on the following dates: February 7th, April 4th, June 6th. If you live abroad it is possible to do an application interview through SKYPE. Click APPLICATION for downloads. Before application please contact: info@master-animation.com

PROFESSIONAL MASTER ANIMATION

The practice of animation is no longer restricted exclusively to the world of cinema. Driven by new technologies, production methods and platforms, innovative forms of animation now reach a broad range of audiences outside the theatre. Animation is playing an increasingly important role in various disciplines of art and design, film, games and interactive media and can also be found in such wide-ranging fields as architecture and science.

AKV\St.Joost*, School of Fine Art and Design (Breda, The Netherlands) now offers a one year Masters Course in PROFESSIONAL ANIMATION**. The course offers you the opportunity to further develop your artistic identity and to position yourself in a fast moving field.

The one year programme consists of workshops, guest lectures, practical design studies, research and theory. Personal entrepreneurship and networking activities - such as expertpresentations, studio visits and masterclasses all form part of the

---

INFORMATION
PROGRAM / EVENTS
APPLICATION
CONTACT
SHOWCASE
ABOUT US
PARTNERS

MASTER ANIMATION
avans hogeschool
akv|st|joost

XSENS DEMO, November 25

Xsens Technologies demonstrates their MVR motion capture suit on Thursday 25th of November. The master students will then work with the system and produce several demo's in collaboration with bachelors.

MASTER at HAFF

Students and staff of the master Animation gave presentations at the Dutch Animation Film Festival, (HAFF 2010), Nov. 4 & 6, Theater Kikker, Utrecht.

INFORMATION
PROGRAM / EVENTS
APPLICATION
CONTACT
SHOWCASE
ABOUT US
PARTNERS

MASTER ANIMATION
avans hogeschool
akv|st|joost

How to apply:

Step 1: Get in contact

Interested in our masters course? Send us an e-mail via info@master-animation.com

Step 2: Let's meet!

After getting in contact you can come to the academy* to show us some work and tell us your ambitions. If your ambition and talent fits our program, you should fill in an application form.

*If you are living abroad we can use skype / online portfolio

Step 3: Apply

After receiving the application-form we will invite you to meet our selection committee. Convince them and get selected!

You can download an application-form here:

NL

ENG

To be eligible for admission to the postgraduate and master courses Post-St.Joost you must hold a bachelor diploma in Fine Art and/or Design, or have achieved a comparable standard of work through experience.

The academic year for the Professional Master Animation starts in September. The deadline for applications is July the 1st of the same year. Admissions take place at several moments in the year. Foreign applicants are also welcome to apply. Instructions are in Dutch and English.

INFORMATION
PROGRAM / EVENTS
APPLICATION
CONTACT
SHOWCASE
ABOUT US
PARTNERS

MASTER ANIMATION
avans hogeschool
akv|st|joost

Teachers & Staff

Confirmed guest lecturers for 2010-2011

Fons Schiedon (guest lecturer)

Fons Schiedon is one of the guestlecturers for 2010-2011. He's going to enrich the study program with a workshop characterdesign. The results of this workshop will be presented at PLAYGROUNDSFESTIVAL (Oct. 2010)

Claire Spencer Cook (e-coach)

Claire Cook is a Senior Producer / curator at onedotzero (London, UK). She will attend the master-program for 2010-2010 as e-coach. By means of video-conference and blogging Claire will support the students in their personal development and can help them to access an

---

INFORMATION
PROGRAM / EVENTS
APPLICATION
CONTACT
SHOWCASE
ABOUT US
PARTNERS

MASTER ANIMATION
avans hogeschool
akv|st|joost

International Film Festival Breda   starters lift

onedotzero   Animatie

Audiovisueel   xsens

PLAY Grounds

One Show
Five Hundred
Exhibitors
Leeds College of Art & Design
End of Year Show 2007
25th–27th June
Michael
Barrington, Laura Fullbrook,
Charlotte Kiernan, Stephanie Turner, Philip
Tarry, Rachel Austwick, Andrew Dobbie, James Ashworth,
Leigh Unwin, Katherine Hobbis, Samuel Walsh, Jamie Kazemi,
Joseph Gleeson, Arran Mahony, James Seymour, James Wright, Jonathan
Hawkin, Daniel Prince, Paul Hunter, Martin Sumner, Soren Stendevad, Philip
Craske, Kathia Fiaschi, William Armitage, Craig Bunko, Joe Dutton, William Johnson,
Mohammad Reza Sattarzadeh Amiri, Allister Wormald, Maresa Ible, Shaista Ali, Katie Lok,
Kirsten Burger, Zara Parmar, Seama Mistry, Gillian Cass, Margaret Spence, Howyee Law, Ataur
Khan, Jossette Alcock, Sophie Ghosh, Robert Hatton, Jonathan Gill, Sacha Croasdale, Lyndsey Procter,
Jonathan Rhodes, Jade Slater, Rebekah Johnson, Sameena Azam, Hannah Limbachia, Liam Broadbent,
Nabila Kauser, James Sommerville, Toby Long, Chloe Thompson, Luke Johnson-Jackson, Laura Dowling, Joseph
Layfield, Michaela Bateman, Juliette Hadland, Aimee Watson, Anna Milner, Clare Chapman, Catherine Jones,
Lauren Milner, Micah Harbon, Romany Dear, Sophie Egler, Olivia Mulholland, Kirsty Taylor, Kimberley Welsh, Laxmi
Mistry, Jason Crabbe, Jessica Falcus, James Wright, Charlotte Smith, Joe Savery, Ian Hinchliffe, Gillian Griffiths, Michael
Holmes, Natalie Haigh, Ben Cleworth, Adam King, Jamie Roberts, Jacob Close, Amelia Higney, Christopher Hopkinson,
Matthew Lister, Matthew Green, Joseph Finister, Jamie McIntyre, Emily Tosh, James Farlam, Sarah Rhodes, Kelly Lancashire,
Rachel Airy, Sophie Braithwaite, Alexander Harrison, Tony Railton, Rebecca Wilkinson, Cally Bilbey, Megan Robinson, Amie
Hackney, Rosetta Golton, Kyle Horn, James Nicholls, Luke Musharbash, Rowan Briscoe, Jade Ourique, Sophie Fodden, Linda Rainford,
Rachel Bennett, Jonathan Chapman, Joanne Moscrop, Elizabeth Smith, Leanne Mangan, Nicola Cleaver, Megan Jones, Paul Burton,
Laura Pointon, Jade Anderson, Emily Beaumont, Amardeep Bilkhu, Laura Chalk, Stephanie Cockcroft, Alice Cockerham, Chelsea Hale,
Chloe Hodgson, Karenjeet Kaur, Rose Killin, Amanda Leather, Jodie Lindus, Rhiannan Malko, Lisa Morley, Charlene Prust, Laura Quantrill,
Sally Roden, Eleanor Slade, Claire Slaney, Hattie Spowage, Darecca Stainforth, Emma Steele, Jodie Taylor, Charlie Thackray, Hannah
Tomlinson, Heather Ugarte, Luke Hoyes, Paul Olivier, Simon Green, Richard Jennings, Adam Feeney, Carl Mortimer, Christopher Brearley,
Adam Buchanan, Thomas Horner, Harnekh Bhakar, Brenda Hollweg, Asheeba Charles, Andrew Cochrane, James Brown, Lucy Parkin, Gemma
Burke, Leanne Clark, Olivia Deligianni, Charlotte Draycott, William Edmond, Jonathan Epps, Catherine Farrell, Hayley Gardner, Rebecca
Hutchinson, Ella Johnston, Alexandra Keane, Catherine Lamb, David Lindsay, Thomas Martin, Hannah McGowan, Robert Middleton, Charlotte
Moss, Claire Perry, Nicky Rai, Claire Roberson, Rebecca Sykes, Michael Ward, Kirsty Wilson, James Richards, Scott Colley, Kayleigh Senior, Alex
Young, Claire Fisher, Oliver Shaw, William De Biasio, Alexander Moody, Aidan Mayne, Haydn Robinson, Gail Battye, Dalveer Sohal, Solomon Francis,
Karl Cartwright, Robert McCrimmon, William Schofield, Faye Cunningham, Edward Kastin, Bethany Crossley, Chris Walker, Hannah Sadler, Arron
Playfoot, Sianne Young, Isra Butt, Victoria Jablonski, Emily Berckley, Jessica Mitchell, Mandeep Mann, Lloyd Parker, Hayley Scott, Sara Neuberg,
Louise Elliott, Sophie Daysh, Richard Phillips, Rosanne Smith, Danielle Erdinc, Jessica Cave, Kathryn Bacon, Christopher Ensell, Francesca Lane,
Craig MacAuley, Jody Holliday, Lucy Wood, Judy Kessler, Jessica Copsey, Amy Walker, Sarah Covington, Oliver O'Driscoll, Ashanti Harris, Katie
Schofield, Claire Walker, Celina Joyce, Hoi-Kam Chan, Grace Turner, Nina Beresford, Jonathan Ward, Claire Rafter, Rosemarie Wachsmuth, Cassandra
Gomersall, Runa Begum, Laurence Brown, Caroline Restrick, Tiaz Taylor, Stephen Gouldin, Anna Turner, Lindsay Christie, Neil Grandy, John Withey,
Ann Barrett, Helen Briggs, Kiranjit Kaur, Natasha Adams, Melanie Kalay, Amber Wilson, Sam Rush, Geni Spoors, Rachael Jenkins, Victoria Wilson,
Laura Armstrong, Sophie Smith, Tracy Dawson, Gemma Ramage, Lisa Marsden, Bethany Hunter, Stephanie Brough, Kathryn Armitage, Lydia Townsend,
Ruby Hepburn, Stella Cecil, Elizabeth Harrison, Eleanor Charlton, Sonia Malik, Kirby Frisby, Leonie Wilson, Olivia Palamountain, Nadja Sundberg,
Elizabeth Robson, Susan Bradshaw, Elizabeth Cousley, Linda Hutchinson, Jennifer Roberts, Harriet Steele, Catherine Neumann, Debbie Raine, Judith
Sims, Elizabeth Pennock, Justine Bradley, James Appleyard, William House, Amelia Wood, Lisa Macbeth, Joseph Creffield, Ivana Kolcabova, Murina
Marsden, Christine Hinchliffe, Kelly Bruce, Kay Patel, Paul Ashton, Ophelia Yook, Ailsa Amos, Damien Guy, Caroline Tsang, Elizabeth Riordan,
Robert Smith, Ian Crewe, Sarah Johnson, Anna Fox, Stuart Perry, Amy Adamson, Thandiwe Ndlovu, Sany Cristovao, Robert McGregor, James
McGrath, Scott Thomson, Emma Bosworth, Heather Dovey, Suzanne Elanis, Kirsty Kaye, Rahima Ali, Sofia Palenzuela, Lee McKenzie, Dean Wood,
Kirk Williams, Charlotte Taylor, Melissa Petch, Adriana Georgescu, Cyrielle Pailloux, Gill Bage, Joanne Williams, Phillipa Wilkinson, Richard
Bryant, Helena Janeckova, Katherine Robinson, Matthew Fletcher, Payam Abdollahzadeh, Angie Khupe, Daniel Khammo, Nadia Burgess, Sahar
Rahbar, Mandy Hudson, Claire Bray, Shaun Barker-Newton, Fiona Winter, Christine Golton, Hayley Wilson, Samantha Maltas, Ailsa Read,
Jacqueline Runton, Tasleem Fazal, Grace Sugden, Dawn Broughton, Maria Gunn, Jonathan Hinds, Bernard Midgley, Estefania Lera Sanchez,
Alex Chan, Rachel Schofield, Louise Abbott, Dominique Brown, Lori Campbell, Joanna Eddy, Claudia Glickman, Hayley Jennison, Charlotte
Johnson, Kerrie Lawrence, Rosanna Lilly, Limor Morris, Helen Richardson, Lisa Stern, John Stroish, Nadia Tareen, Samantha Venner,
William Walsh, Joanne Pailing, Clare Wild, Samantha Taylor, Clover Robin, Susanna Ash, Hannah Wharam, Charlotte Ingman-White,
Joanna Greenan, Joanna Vallis, Emily Morris, Rosalind Wear, Sophie Websdale, Emma Prescott, Kathryn Dooley, Iona Baird, Leanne
Bean, Elizabeth Custance, Rachel Brier, Kuljinder Nagra, Kerry Thomas, Emily Wagstaff, Laura Bailey, Heather Roberts, Nicola
Strathearn, Reema Desai, Bethan Read, Holly Robinson, Sarah Robinson, Amanda Simmons, Charlotte Booth, Liane Walton, Alex
Glew, Katie Barrett, Catherine Johnson, Hester Simpson, Samantha Wong, Jillian Smith, Jake Collinson-Lawrence, Holly Anker,
Caroline Sims, Tanya Scott, Lydia Smith, Annabel Carter, Victoria Exton, Emma Bailey, Anna Iantorno, Bushra Bodla, Carol
Cook, Amy Purnell, Cheryl Whitehead, Aysha Alton, Emily Finn, Sarah Johnson, Liam Jefferies, Sarah Gough, Donna Walker,
Sarah Barrett, Holly Banks, Tracey Pinder, Kate Harrison, Bhavit Shah, Richard Martin, Bryony Pritchard, Kelly Pollard,
Gemma Fozzard, Nicola Middleton, Sophie Strong, Kate Barton, Helen Williams, Adam Hayward, Fiona Murray, Caroline
Lodge, Rose Thompson, Catherine Hempton, Alicia Talikowska, Luis Sousa, Claire Duffin, Joseph Critchley, James
Shaw, Joanne Fox, Michael Moore, Thomas Minns, Nicholas Edwards, Christopher Duffy, Sina Becker, Gordon
Edwards, Beverley Mitton, Michael Schofield, Joel Standeven, Lyndsey Slaven, Emma Smith, Jessica Pamphlett,
Claire McKeand, Michael Clarke, Angharad Cooper, Andrew Lamb, Juanita Wray, Laura Tait, Richard
Bendelow, William Potts, Thomas Hudson, Christopher Mackenzie, Danielle Shepherd, Caroline
Cutner, Luke Rothery, Miriam Balieiro Terzich, James Griffin, Rebecca Krinks, Mark Wood,
Jack Saunders, Jason Cover, Lawrence Brown, Stacey Wormald, Daljeet Riyat, Ceri Allen,
Eleanor Brown, Jonathan Erazo, Frank Lloyd-Platt, Neil Parkinson, Sophie Marks,
Nathan Dickens, David Beales, Lisa McKay, Salimeh Salimiyan, Alison Pickup,
Nicola Bell, Lisa Wilmot, Rebecca Baker, Katie Ardron, Saima Nadeem,
Rachael Bowles, Charlotte Williamson, Benjamin Bostock,
Camille Marquestaut, Thomas Plaskitt, Adrian
Whipp, Claire Paul, Charlotte Midgley,
Julia Lee.
Tel 0113 202 8000
info@leeds-art.ac.uk
www.leeds-art.ac.uk
LEEDS COLLEGE OF ART & DESIGN

main reason for choosing justified alignment. There are some occasions when hyphenation is unavoidable, such as in scientific or legal texts where long technical or subject-specific words are common. Some foreign languages also have a higher-than-average proportion of long words. For example, the German for maximum speed limit is "Hoechsgeschwindigkeitsbegrenzung," which would probably need to be hyphenated even if it began in the middle of a line. Ragged-right or ragged-left body text usually looks ugly when words at the ends of lines are hyphenated and it doesn't help with readability.

Pitfall: Do not use forced justification, where short lines at the ends of paragraphs are forced to spread across the column measure, unless you are deliberately trying to achieve an unusual effect.

Pitfall: Unless you want to include hyphenation, check that auto-hyphenation is disabled before you set body text. It is the default setting in most design programs.

While on the subject of paragraph endings, other obstacles to readability include widows and orphans. A widow is one short word on the line at the end of a paragraph. This has the distracting effect of seeming to increase the amount of space between paragraphs. An orphan can be either the first line of a paragraph falling at the bottom of a column of text or the last line falling at the top of a column. Like widows, orphans stand alone, looking abandoned, which is distracting to the reader.

Transitions between paragraphs of text are usually indicated by an increased linespace or a space before the first word of the new paragraph, known as an indent. As with widows and orphans, these spaces may cause visual disturbance but they may also be used to good effect.

This column of text has been set in Caslon 6 point on 7 point leading. The text has been justified so that the lines of text are parallel with the column edges. The text has been hyphenated to allow for more even wordspacing across the justified text. Hyphenation is often necessary when the text contains words that have a lot of characters such as the German word for maximum speed limit, which is Hoechsgeschwindigkeitsbegrenzung, mentioned in the text.

This column of text has been set in Caslon 6 point on 7 point leading. In this example, the text has not been justified but has been set ranged left so that the lines of text align with the left edge of the column. The text has not been hyphenated. As you can see, Hoechsgeschwindigkeitsbegrenzung has been pushed down to the next line. The words are more evenly spaced in this column of text, which makes them easier to read.

A widow is a short word which drops down to the last line of a paragraph. It stands alone, and looks separate from the rest of the paragraph. In this example the widow is the widow.

An orphan is a line from the beginning of a paragraph that has been left on its own at the bottom of a column while the rest of the paragraph has moved to the second column of text. It may also be a line from the end of a paragraph that has strayed onto the top of the next column of the grid.

It is worth checking your text each time you make an adjustment, to ensure that you have not inadvertently made a widow or an orphan.

top: This example contrasts hyphenated justified text with unhyphenated ranged-left text. Many designers would argue that the left alignment without hyphenation is easier to read than the justified type with hyphenation. However, this is a subjective matter and often depends on what looks right in individual circumstances.

above: Typographic widows and orphans, as shown in this example, should be avoided.

below: KalleGraphics have indicated paragraph breaks by an indent on the first line of each paragraph.

Layout

There are specific issues relating to using text in layout, such as structure, tone, white space, balance, and the relationship between type and image.

Grids

Columns of text form grids and these define the structure of a layout. All the factors relating to paragraphs are important when designing a grid. You should also have a typeface, or range of typefaces, and size of type in mind. It is difficult to visualize how a typeface will perform in a grid unless you have already tried it, so it is useful to collect examples of different typefaces used in a variety of grid structures. For example, try a serif (e.g. Palatino) and a sans serif (e.g. Univers) typeface at 9 point in a range of leadings in a two-, three-, and four-column grid on a letter-size layout.

Shades of gray

Decisions such as the choice of typeface and grid and the amount of leading and tracking to be applied affect the density of body text on the page. Density is also referred to as the color of the text and can affect the layout as well as emphasis and relationship with any images. The color of the text needs to be considered in relation to the tone of any images incorporated in the layout. The diagram right shows the way that the color of body text can be affected by different linespacing and how this property can be harnessed to create layers or hierarchies of information (see also chapter 5).

This text is set in 5 point Univers 55 Roman on 5 point leading. This text is set in 5 point Univers 55 Roman on 5 point leading. This text is set in 5 point Univers 55 Roman on 5 point leading. This text is set in 5 point Univers 55 Roman on 5 point leading. This text is set in 5 point Univers 55 Roman on 5 point leading.

This text is set in 5 point Univers 55 Roman on 6 point leading. This text is set in 5 point Univers 55 Roman on 6 point leading. This text is set in 5 point Univers 55 Roman on 6 point leading. This text is set in 5 point Univers 55 Roman on 6 point leading. This text is set in 5 point Univers 55 Roman on 6 point leading.

This text is set in 5 point Univers 55 Roman on 7 point leading. This text is set in 5 point Univers 55 Roman on 7 point leading. This text is set in 5 point Univers 55 Roman on 7 point leading. This text is set in 5 point Univers 55 Roman on 7 point leading. This text is set in 5 point Univers 55 Roman on 7 point leading.

This text is set in 5 point Univers 55 Roman on 8 point leading. This text is set in 5 point Univers 55 Roman on 8 point leading. This text is set in 5 point Univers 55 Roman on 8 point leading. This text is set in 5 point Univers 55 Roman on 8 point leading.

This text is set in 5 point Palatino Regular on 8 point leading. This text is set in 5 point Palatino Regular on 8 point leading. This text is set in 5 point Palatino Regular on 8 point leading. This text is set in 5 point Palatino Regular on 8 point leading. This text is set in 5 point Palatino Regular on 8 point leading.

This text is set in 5 point Palatino Regular on 7 point leading. This text is set in 5 point Palatino Regular on 7 point leading. This text is set in 5 point Palatino Regular on 7 point leading. This text is set in 5 point Palatino Regular on 7 point leading. This text is set in 5 point Palatino Regular on 7 point leading.

This text is set in 5 point Palatino Regular on 6 point leading. This text is set in 5 point Palatino Regular on 6 point leading. This text is set in 5 point Palatino Regular on 6 point leading. This text is set in 5 point Palatino Regular on 6 point leading. This text is set in 5 point Palatino Regular on 6 point leading.

This text is set in 5 point Palatino Regular on 5 point leading. This text is set in 5 point Palatino Regular on 5 point leading. This text is set in 5 point Palatino Regular on 5 point leading. This text is set in 5 point Palatino Regular on 5 point leading. This text is set in 5 point Palatino Regular on 5 point leading.

Palatino and Univers typefaces at 5-, 6-, 7-, and 8-point leadings on a four-column grid. Different typefaces and paragraph formats look very different in contrasting grid structures.

Mina Arko demonstrates the difference in text color that may be achieved with variations in linespacing and point size.

Activity

Select sections of body text from newspapers and magazines—choose examples that have different leading, type weight, etc. so that you have a range of body-text colors. Cut the examples into blocks approximately 1–1½ inches high and 2–3 inches wide. Arrange the sections so that they go from a light tone to a dark one. Next, experiment with tonal difference by making a "type face" using sections of found body text. To do this, either take a photo of a face or find an existing portrait and trace around the different tonal areas then replace these with sections of body text of similar tonal value (color). Having experimented with found text, try drawing the portrait using individual letterforms to create the tonal variations.

above: A student selects different sections of printed text to demonstrate the range of tones achieved with different settings such as leading.

right: Having collected snippets displaying a wide range of body-text colors, the student arranges them, cutting to shape where necessary, to create the tone in this portrait.

left: Default Bangkok have filled all available space with type to make a strong visual impact for this label design.

below: Inksurge have created an asymmetrical but well-balanced composition for this poster. The small colored blocks of text at the bottom right are surrounded with white space, which balances the heavier text and slabs of color at the top left.

White space

White space, the portion of the page left unmarked, is an important consideration in design. It provides breathing space for information, separates sections of information, and can give a feeling of opulence and sophistication because it demonstrates an unconstrained use of materials. A good example of this is the use of generous margins and/or leading in some upscale magazines and webpages. Lack of white space can cause a design to look compacted and, in some circumstances, low in quality. It is therefore important to bear in mind the content to be communicated when making decisions about white space. (N.B. if the plain background on a page is in a color other than white it is still referred to as white space.)

Symmetry and asymmetry

The overall shape that blocks of text, titles, and images form on the page can be used as a design feature or as an aid to communication. Deciding what kind of message you want your layout to deliver can be a useful point of departure in design. A symmetrical layout is one where, if you drew a vertical line down the center of the layout, the portion on the right-hand side of the line would be, roughly speaking, a mirror image of the left-hand portion. Asymmetry occurs when the two sides of the layout contrast with each other. When using asymmetry you may choose to balance the weight of each side equally or have an imbalance, which can make a design look quite edgy. A symmetrical layout can be used to convey a message of stability and reassurance, whereas an asymmetrical layout might communicate dynamism or controversy.

Letman used hand lettering for this symmetrical poster design that reflects the symmetry of the body.

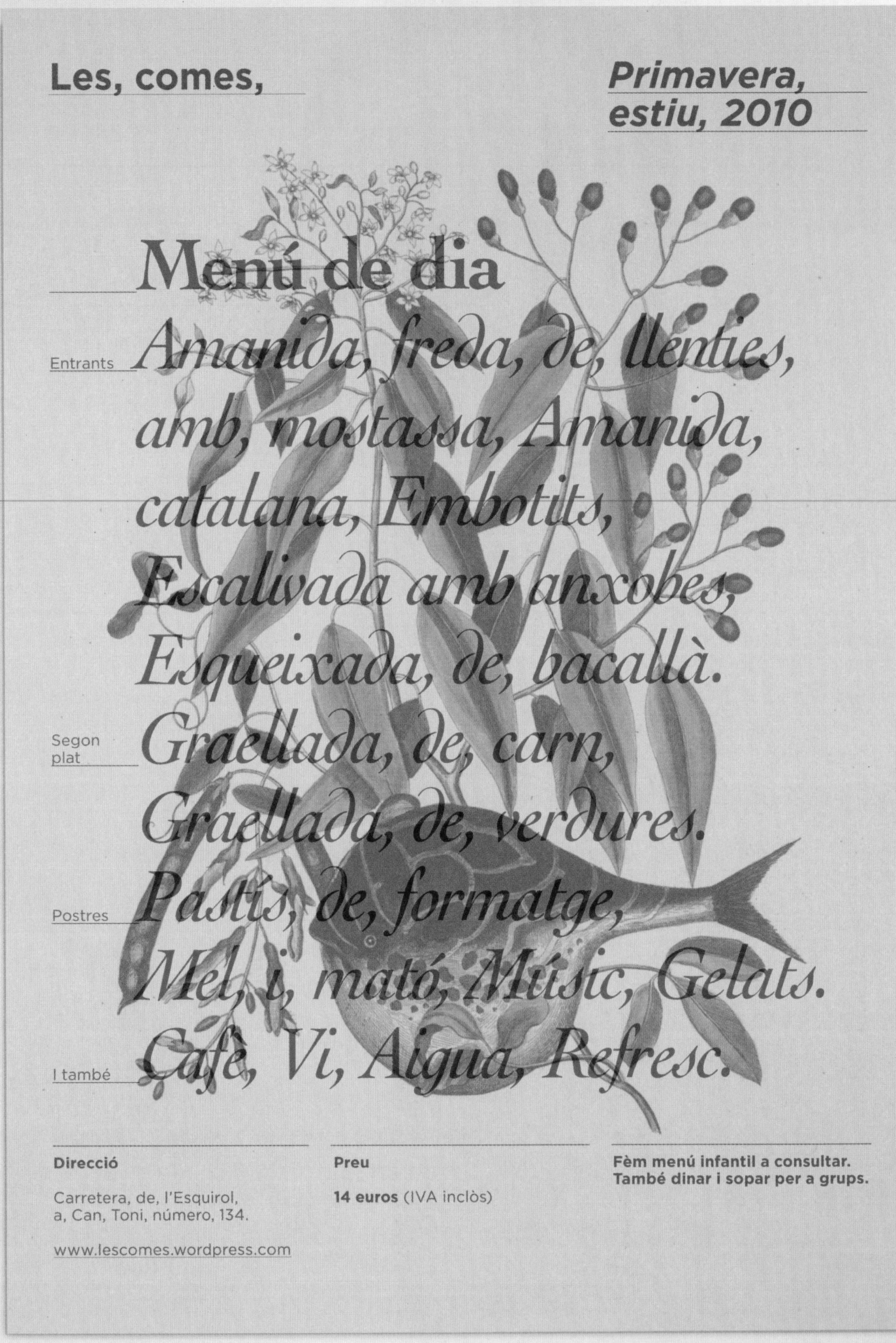

Menú de dia

Entrants — *Amanida, freda, de, llenties, amb, mostassa, Amanida, catalana, Embotits, Escalivada amb anxoves, Esqueixada, de, bacallà.*

Segon plat — *Graellada, de, carn, Graellada, de, verdures.*

Postres — *Pastís, de, formatge, Mel, i, mató, Músic, Gelats.*

I també — *Cafè, Vi, Aigua, Refresc.*

Direcció

Carretera, de, l'Esquirol, a, Can, Toni, número, 134.

www.lescomes.wordpress.com

Preu

14 euros (IVA inclòs)

**Fèm menú infantil a consultar.
També dinar i sopar per a grups.**

opposite: Jordi Serra Santano has laid lines of text over images that relate to the culinary theme of this menu.

above: Mina Arko has replicated the shape of the feather, on the right, in the shape of the body text to give a balanced feel to the layout for this double-page spread.

Type and image

Although this book primarily discusses the use of type, images cannot be ignored because they form an integral part of many layouts. Where blocks of type and images are combined in a layout, it is important to consider how they sit together visually. For example, an image on the right-hand page of a double-page spread that indicates some sort of visual leftward direction can help to lead the reader to the beginning of the text on the left-hand page.

Pitfall: When placing images with text, it is important to position an image on the same page as the text it relates to or, if this isn't possible, ensure that the link is clearly signposted.

Type, or sections of type, may be treated as image and may be custom-made for a specific design or taken from special typefaces known as ornaments, dingbats, symbols, or borders. There is a large range of these available, some of which are traditional, based on those created by 18th-century type designers such as Pierre Simon Fournier (le Jeune).

left: Official Classic Ltd. have used ornaments and symbols as decoration on the advertisement for their typeface Solaria.

below: Monotype have produced an Arabic-influenced set of type ornaments, Arabesque.

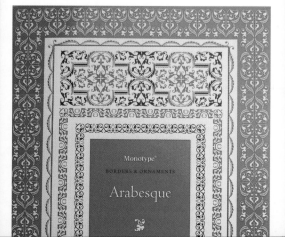

"That part of my life I cannot remember, between 2007–2010, no—between 2006–2009."

In this example, an en-dash has been used to indicate ranges of dates and an em-dash has been used to indicate a pause.

Graphic elements

There are other graphic devices in the type designer's toolbox. These include various styles of rules (lines), graphic symbols, and ornaments such as arrows and stars, initial and drop caps, and punctuation such as exclamation marks and dashes. Dashes are not the same as hyphens. They have various functions, such as indicating a pause, a parenthesis, or a range of numbers, and they come in two forms: em-dashes, which are the width of a capital "M," and en-dashes, which are traditionally half the width of an em-dash (but nowadays tend to be slightly wider than this). When indicating a pause or parenthesis, the usual style for US English is an unspaced em-dash, and for UK English, an en-dash with a space either side.

Many other languages feature special characters, such as umlauts (ü) in German and cedillas (ç) in French, which may be exploited as design features. Some special characters have been appropriated for use on website addresses such as the symbol for at (@) and the tilde (~). Another graphic device that appears regularly on e-mails and blogs is the emoticon, which may be produced either using punctuation (;-o) or by importing a customized symbol such as ☺.

Ligatures

Needing slightly more explanation are ligatures. These are where two letterforms are conjoined to form a distinctive shape, such as the Icelandic æ. Ligatures developed from the need to condense text in early hand-produced manuscripts to save on labor and materials.

NINE MEN ON THE MOON

Quickfire

Rock & Roll!

Livius Dietzel and HVD Fonts produced a set of ligatures for the typeface Livory, some of which are demonstrated in this promotional piece.

Amnesty Aktion magazine
by Fons Hickmann m23, Berlin

Amnesty Aktion communicates information about selected Amnesty International activities. Each issue contains a double-page spread that displays statistics, illustrates the international significance of certain processes, and calls for active participation. The magazine needs to be cost-efficient and quick to produce, but still make an impact.

The art direction was by Prof. Fons Hickmann and Gesine Grotrian-Steinweg. The magazine was produced in four-color offset litho across eight pages.

Fons Hickmann used capital letters with deep linespacing to give this design a more spacious feel incorporating white space. The design is asymmetrical, with the logo at the bottom right helping to balance the layout.

AMNESTY INTERNATIONAL AUSGABE 02/2006

amnestyAKTION

MITMACHEN
Keine Geheimflüge im Namen der Terrorismusbekämpfung!

STIRN BIETEN
Der ai-Jahresbericht 2006

SUDAN
Massenvergewaltigungen als Kriegswaffe

ABGEFAHREN
Für amnesty um die Welt

MEHRERE HUNDERT MENSCHEN SIND SEIT 2001 VON DER CIA ALS GEFANGENE ÜBER LÄNDERGRENZEN HINWEG VERSCHLEPPT WORDEN.

ai
amnesty international
FÜR DIE MENSCHENRECHTE

right. This cover design uses all capital letters, but in different sizes to provide hierarchy in a predominantly symmetrical layout.

Far right: On this cover Fons Hickmann experiment with legibility, with the wavy background pattern integrated into the type. The text is still legible even though some elements, such as umlauts, are nearly obscured.

Below: In this double-page spread, hierarchy has been established using different sizes of type as well as different colors for headings and highlighted sections of text. This is reinforced by the use of justified and ranged left alignment to distinguish between types of information. The strong grid, good use of white space, and careful alignment of images with the type gives an organized, clean feel. This contrasts with a dynamic use of large graphic symbols across the double-page spread.

amnesty**AKTION**

ARTIKEL EINS

FREI GLEICH BRÜDERLICHKEIT

ALLE MENSCHEN SIND FREI UND GLEICH AN WÜRDE UND RECHTEN GEBOREN. SIE SIND MIT VERNUNFT UND GEWISSEN BEGABT UND SOLLEN EINANDER IM GEISTE DER BRÜDERLICHKEIT BEGEGNEN.

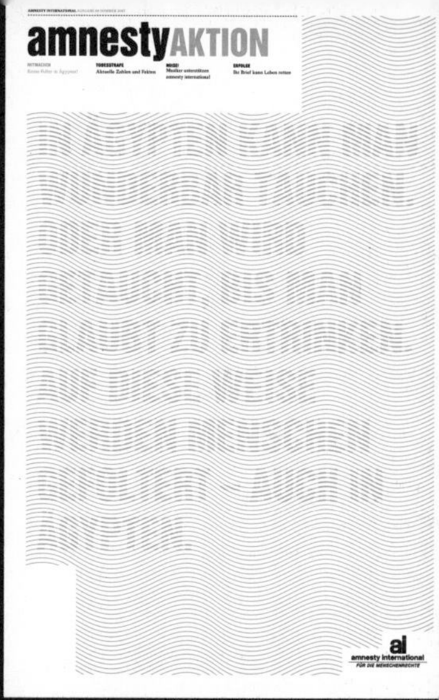

amnesty**AKTION**

MITMACHEN   AMNESTY AKTION 84

EINSATZ FÜR DIE MENSCHEN-RECHTE – EIN ZEICHEN SETZEN

©Chinese Pen Center (ICPC)   ©Catherine Berthillier, Galerie P.   ©Joana C. Fernández Nunez

Unter diesem Motto startet amnesty international am 10. Dezember, dem internationalen Tag der Menschenrechte, breit angelegte Aktionen für Personen, die massiv von Menschenrechtsverletzungen betroffen sind. EinSatz heißt: Schon ein Satz, den Sie schreiben, kann einem anderen Menschen helfen. EinSatz bedeutet auch: Einsatz für die Menschenrechte anderer.

Jeder von uns schreibt E-Mails. Jeden Tag. Menschen „chatten", „googeln" oder „mailen" aus allen Teilen, in alle Teile der Welt. Und manchmal bleibt ein Mensch in der Maschen das weltweite Netzes hängen. Zum Beispiel der 37-jährige Journalist und Dichter Shi Tao. Er schrieb am 20. April 2004 eine E-Mail, die ihn teuer zu stehen kam.

Zu diesem Zeitpunkt arbeitete er bei einer Zeitung in der chinesischen Provinz Hunan. Auf einer Redaktionssitzung, kurz vor dem 15. Jahrestag der blutigen Niederschlagung der Studentendemonstration auf dem Tiananmen-Platz in Peking, wurden die Redakteure über eine neue Richtlinie der Kommunistischen Partei (KPCh) informiert. Diese sah strikte Verhaltensmaßregeln bei der Berichterstattung am Jahrestag vor. Die Partei „wertete" Medienvertreter vor möglichen sozialen Unruhen und der Unterwanderung durch „demokratische Kräfte und feindliche ausländische Elemente" und forderte sie auf, „vorbeugende Maßnahmen" zu ergreifen. Journalisten wurden angewiesen, „die öffentliche Meinung korrigierend zu beeinflussen", „keine Meinungen, die der zentralen Politik zuwider liefen, zu veröffentlichen" und „ihre Aufgaben zu ihrem Arbeitsschwerpunkt zu machen. Worüber sollten sie Kollegen, die verdächtige Kontakte mit „demokratischen Elementen am Übersee" unterhielten, bei den Behörden zur Anzeige bringen. Shi Tao führte bei der Sitzung Protokoll und sandte es anonym über seinen Yahoo-Account an einen Mitarbeiter der Stiftung „Asia Democracy" mit Sitz in New York. Noch am selben Tag wurden seine Mitteilungen unter einem Pseudonym im „Democracy Forum", das sich für die Demokratie in China einsetzt, veröffentlicht. An den Folgetagen veröffentlichten auch anderen ausländische Webseiten Taos Informationen.

Am 24. November 2004 verhafteten Sicherheitskräfte Shi Tao in der Nähe seiner Wohnung und beschlagnahmten Computer und Laptop. Am 31. Januar 2005 klagte man ihn offiziell wegen „Weitergabe von Staatsgeheimnissen" an. Sein Internet-Anbieter Yahoo, der in einem Vertrag mit den chinesischen Behörden deren drastische Zensurmaßnahmen (faktisch anerkennt, hatte den Standort des Senderechputers herausgefunden und an die chinesischen Ermittler weitergegeben.

Nun verbüßt Shi Tao im Gefängnis von Changsha eine zehnjährige Haftstrafe und muss Zwangsarbeit leisten. Er stellt Schmuckstücke her und leidet wegen des im Produktionsprozess entstehenden Staubes unter schweren Haut- und Atemwegserkrankungen. Seine Familie ist seit seiner Verhaftung ständiger Schikane ausgesetzt. Sein Ehefrau hielt dem Druck nicht stand und ließ sich von ihm scheiden. Im Februar 2005 startete amnesty international die erste Eilaktion für Shi Tao. Tausende Menschen aus den verschiedenen Ländern forderten seine bedingungslose Freilassung, weil er lediglich sein Recht auf freie Meinungsäußerung in Anspruch genommen hatte.

Eilaktionen von amnesty international sind sehr erfolgreich: In 40 Prozent der Fälle verbessert sich die Situation der Betroffenen. Neben der unmittelbaren Wirkung für einzelne Opfer von Menschenrechtsverletzungen leisten sie einen wichtigen Beitrag dazu, Verstöße gegen die Menschenrechte in Zukunft zu verhindern: Sie zeigen den Regierungen, dass die Weltöffentlichkeit diese wahrnimmt und nicht bereit ist, sie zu dulden. Die Arbeit zugunsten einzelner Personen, die von Menschenrechtsverletzungen bedroht oder betroffen sind, spielt auf der Gründung von amnesty international im Jahr 1961 eine zentrale Rolle. Unter dem Motto „EinSatz für die Menschenrechte – ein Zeichen setzen" wird die deutsche ai-Sektion in den kommenden Monaten verstärkt ihre Arbeit zu diesem Thema in das Licht der Öffentlichkeit rücken und Unterstützungsmöglichkeiten entwickeln, mit denen Sie EinSatz leisten können – einfach, schnell

und effektiv. Denn je mehr Unterschriften für eine Petition gesammelt werden, desto größer ist ihre Wirkung. Je mehr Menschen Appellpostkarten schreiben, desto wirkungsvoller sind sie und desto mehr Druck entfaltet Ihr EinSatz auf die Verantwortlichen von Menschenrechtsverletzungen.

In den nächsten drei Monaten können Sie sich für die Journalisten Shi Tao aus der Volksrepublik China, für Annakurban Amankliftschew und Sapardurdi Chadschijew aus Turkmenistan und für Juan Adolfo Fernández Sainz aus Kuba einsetzen. China – Turkmenistan – Kuba: In allen drei Ländern kann die freie Meinungsäußerung das Ende des Lebens bedeuten.

SETZEN SIE EIN ZEICHEN.

Schreiben Sie für Shi Tao, Annakurban Amanklitschew, Sapardurdi Chadschijew und Juan Adolfo Fernández Sainz eins! Diese Menschen brauchen Ihre Unterstützung und nicht zuletzt die Gefahr, dass sie außerhalb des Gefängnismauern nicht vergessen werden. Appellieren Sie mit uns an die Staatschefs Chinas, Turkmenistans sowie Kubas, diese gewaltlosen politischen Gefangenen nicht länger unrechtmäßig festzuhalten.

Wenn Sie über das Schicksal der vier Gefangenen auf dem Laufenden gehalten werden oder die Kampagne darüber hinaus unterstützen möchten, können Sie sich dem 10.12. unter www.amnesty.de anmelden – wir werden Sie gezielt über neue EinSatz-Möglichkeiten informieren.

ZERRISSENE SEELEN – FOLTEROPFERN HELFEN

AMNESTY INTERNATIONAL SETZT SICH WELTWEIT FÜR MENSCHEN EIN, DIE GEFOLTERT WURDEN. EINE KONKRETE HILFE BESTEHT DARIN, DIE KOSTEN FÜR THERAPIEN IN BEHANDLUNGSZENTREN MIT ZU FINANZIEREN.

In 104 der 150 Staaten, die amnesty international im Jahresbericht 2006 aufführt, die Menschen misshandelt und gefoltert werden. Es hat Gesichter, unmenschlich ist sie immer. Sie trifft nicht nur politische Gefangene oder Oppositionelle. Auch systematische Vergewaltigungen von Frauen sind eine Form der Folter. Zunehmend zählen Angehörige von Minderheiten zu den Folteropfern.

WAS TUT AMNESTY INTERNATIONAL?

– ai deckt Fälle von Folter auf;
– ai sorgt dafür, dass die Öffentlichkeit davon erfährt, um so Druck auf die Verantwortlichen auszuüben;
– ai fordert Regierungen auf und setzt sich für Menschen ein, die von Folter bedroht sind;
– ai setzt sich für die Aufklärung von Menschenrechtsverletzungen

Folter erzeugt neben sichtbaren, körperlichen Verletzungen auch unsichtbare, seelische Leiden wie posttraumatische Störungen, Depressionen, Angstzustände und Konzentrationsschwächen. In die Behandlungszentren für Folteropfer geht es darum, diese körperlichen und seelischen Schäden der gefolterten Menschen mithilfe spezieller Therapien so weit wie möglich überwinden zu helfen.

Dabei werden Traumatherapien, Gesprächspsychotherapien oder Kunsttherapien nach körperlichen Verletzungen mit Behandlung eingesetzt.

Weil eine solche Therapie dauert, hängt vom einzelnen Schicksal der Personen und ihrer Verfassung ab. Oft ist die Behandlung längerfristig angelegt und wird durch eine psychosoziale Begleitung ergänzt, die dabei hilft, die Integration in das umstrittene gesellschaftliche Umfeld zu verbessern. So werden z. B. der Besuch von Sprachkursen, die Wohnungs- und Arbeitssuche, oder auch die Mitgliedschaft in einem örtlichen Verein angeregt und unterstützt.

Das Projekt „Hilfe für die therapeutische Behandlung von Folteropfern" von amnesty international in Deutschland lebt von Spenden, die genau für diesen Zweck verwendet werden. Wir würden uns einen Beitrag dazu leisten, dann körperliche und seelische Schäden der gefolterten Menschen mithilfe spezieller Therapien so weit wie möglich überwunden werden.

UNTERSTÜTZEN SIE DAS PROJEKT „HILFE FÜR DIE THERAPEUTISCHE BHANDLUNG VON FOLTEROPFERN" MIT EINER SPENDE:

SPENDENKONTO
807 0000 901
345 KÖLN
BLZ 370 205 00

AKTIONEN UND ERFOLGE   AMNESTY AKTION 84

KRIEG GEGEN DEN TERROR

DER WEG NACH GUANTÁNAMO BEGINNT IN PAKISTAN

Der britische Staatsbürger Moazzam Begg befand sich am 31. Januar 2002 auf einen ruhigen Abend in seinem Haus in Islamabad/Pakistan. Doch mittlerweile begann für ihn ein dreijähriger Alptraum: „Das erste, was ich spürte, war eine Waffe an meinem Kopf. Sie stülpten mir eine Kapuze über, legten mir Handschellen an und trugen mich zu ihrem Fahrzeug." Die Entführer waren pakistanische und US-amerikanische Sicherheitskräfte. Sie verschleppten ihn zunächst nach Afghanistan und dann nach Guantánamo Bay auf Kuba. Ohne Anklage oder Gerichtsverfahren verbrachte er die meiste Zeit in Einzelhaft, er wurde misshandelt und gefoltert. Drei Jahre später, im Januar 2005, durfte er nach Großbritannien zurückkehren.

Moazzam Begg gehört zu den seit 11. September 2005 Hunderten von Menschen in Pakistan. Die pakistanische Regierung gilt als Hauptverbündete ins von den USA angeführten „Krieg gegen den Terror". Seither sind fast Anzeige eines pakistanischen Militärsprechers rund 500 mutmaßliche Terroristen getötet und mehr als 1.000 Personen festgenommen worden. Betroffene berichten von Isolationshaft und Folter. Häufig fehlt ihnen der Zugang zu einem Rechtsanwalt, Familienangehörige erhalten oft keine Information über den Aufenthaltsort der Betroffenen. Einige wurden in US-Gewahrsam überführen, etliche von ihnen sind später in Guantánamo wieder aufgetaucht – so auch der Bremer Türke Murat Kurnaz, der erst im August dieses Jahres nach mehr als vier Jahren Haft in Guantánamo nach Bremen zurückgekehrt ist. Seine Reise nach Pakistan war Kurnaz zum Verhängnis geworden.

Auch wenn jedes Land das Recht hat, Gefahren abzuwehren und Straftaten zu verfolgen, muss Pakistan beim Vorgehen gegen mutmaßliche Terroristen nationale und internationale Recht beachten. Unter allen Umständen unzulässig sind somit das „Verschwindenlassen" von Menschen, extralegale Hinrichtungen, Haft ohne Anklage, jegliche Misshandlung und Folter sowie die ungesetzliche Auslieferung von Gefangenen in US-Gewahrsam. Daran erinnert der aktuelle Bericht von amnesty international „Pakistan: Human rights ignored in the war on terror". Die Menschenrechtsorganisation weist auf mehr als 100 Seiten zahlreiche Fälle namentlich nach und belegt, dass die Übergriffe zunehmend auf Menschen ausgeweitet werden, die keineswegs terrorverdächtig sind. So finden sich unter den Opfern von Menschenrechtsverletzungen Männer, Frauen und sogar Kinder, dass diese Anhaltspunkte für terroristische Aktivitäten gegen sie vorlagen. Auch Journalisten, die nur über den „Krieg gegen den Terror" berichtet haben, oder medizinisches Personal, das angeblich Terrorverdächtige behandelt haben soll, sind gefährdet.

Weitere Informationen unter www.amnesty.de

AMNESTY INTERNATIONAL KÜRT NELSON MANDELA

©Jürgen Schadeberg

AMNESTY INTERNATIONAL KÜRT NELSON MANDELA ZUM „BOTSCHAFTER DES GEWISSENS".

Der Preis würdigt außergewöhnliche persönliche Beiträge bei der Durchsetzung der Menschenrechte. Der ehemalige Anti-Apartheid-Kämpfer habe „zeit seines Lebens für Freiheit und Gerechtigkeit gekämpft" und sei „mehr als jeder andere lebende Mensch zum Symbol für Hoffnung und Idealismus" geworden, sagte der amnesty-Sprecher Bill Shipsey in Johannesburg. Mandela ist der vierte Empfänger des Preises. Der ehemalige tschechische Präsident Vaclav Havel, die frühere UN-Menschenrechtskommissarin Mary Robinson und die Rockband U2 haben die Auszeichnung bereits bekommen.

WER? WIE? WAS? WIESO? WESHALB? WARUM?

©ai

DIE „ALLGEMEINE ERKLÄRUNG DER MENSCHENRECHTE" FÜR KINDER

Am 10. Dezember 1948 trafen sich die Mitgliedsländer der Vereinten Nationen in New York und verkündeten auf ihrer Generalversammlung die „Allgemeine Erklärung der Menschenrechte". In 30 Artikeln sind diese grundlegenden Rechte aller Menschen genau festgelegt. Für die Menschenrechtsorganisation amnesty international sind die Artikel Grundlage ihrer Arbeit. Damit diese Rechte weltweit geachtet werden, nur wenn alle Menschen frei aufwachsen können, wenn jeder gleichermaßen als wertvoll anerkannt wird und Männer, Frauen und Kinder ohne Angst vor Strafe denken, glauben und sagen können, was sie wollen, ist ein friedliches Leben miteinander möglich. Um allen Kindern diese Rechte bereits im Grundschulalter bekannt zu machen und nahe zu bringen, hat ai alle 30 Artikel der Menschenrechte mit einer für Kinder verständlichen Sprache und mit entsprechenden Illustrationen versehen.

Broschüre für Kinder von 6-10 Jahren
14 x 14 cm, 48 Seiten, vierfarbig
Illustration: Yayo Kawamura, Berlin
Text: Sibylle Rieckhoff, Kinderbuchautorin, Hamburg
Preis: 9.00 Euro (Mengenrabatt auf Anfrage möglich)
Zu bestellen unter: versand@amnesty.de oder per Post: amnesty international, 53108 Bonn (Versand)

IHR BRIEF KANN LEBEN RETTEN

Nichts fürchten Staaten mehr, als dass ihre Menschenrechtsverletzungen ins Licht der Öffentlichkeit gezerrt werden. Deshalb hat amnesty international das Frühwarnsystem der Urgent Actions entwickelt. Diese Eilaktionen haben bereits Tausenden von Menschen das Leben gerettet. Urgent Actions funktionieren nach einem einfachen Prinzip: Sie brauchen nur einen Brief zu schreiben.

Immer wenn amnesty international von willkürlichen Festnahmen, „Verschwindenlassen", Misshandlungen oder drohenden Folterungen oder Hinrichtungen erfährt, wird eine Urgent Action gestartet. amnesty international ruft dann weltweit dazu auf, an die verantwortlichen Regierungen zu appellieren, drohende Menschenrechtsverletzungen zu unterbinden. Beteiligen sich Sie sich an den Urgent Actions, denn Ihr Brief kann Leben retten!

VR CHINA: SCHÜSSE AUF TIBETISCHE FLÜCHTLINGE

Eine internationale Bergsteigergruppe wurde am 30. September 2006 im Himalayagebirge unweit des Mount Everest Zeuge, wie chinesische Grenzposten auf eine Gruppe Tibeter geschossen haben, die nach Nepal fliehen wollten. Unter den Tibetern befanden sich auch Kinder und Jugendliche, von denen mindestens zwei – ein 13-jähriger Junge und die Nonne Kelsang Namtso – vermutlich getötet worden sind. Neun Kinder im Alter von etwa sechs bis zehn Jahren sowie ein Mann sollen von den chinesischen Behörden festgenommen worden sein, und von 20 weiteren Personen fehlt jede Spur. amnesty international in daher um die Sicherheit der Inhaftierten und Verschollenen besorgt. Schreiben Sie an den chinesischen Ministerpräsidenten und verurteilen Sie das gewaltsame Beschuss von Flüchtlingen durch chinesische Grenztruppen. Fordern Sie die chinesische Regierung auf, die näheren Umstände des Zwischenfalls umgehend aufzuklären und offenzulegen sowie die Handlungen der beteiligten Sicherheitskräfte zu überprüfen und die Verantwortlichen gegebenenfalls vor Gericht zu stellen.

RICHTEN SIE IHREN APPELL AN DEN CHINESISCHEN MINISTERPRÄSIDENTEN:
Wen Jiabao Guojia Zongli,
Guowuyuan,
9 Xihuangchang Gerbeiju, Beijingshi 100032,
Volksrepublik China

Weitere Informationen finden Sie unter www.amnesty.de/ua

EILAKTIONEN VON AMNESTY INTERNATIONAL WIRKEN

Peru: amnesty international startete im Mai 2006 eine Eilaktion zugunsten der beiden ehemaligen gewaltlosen politischen Gefangenen Herminio Palomino Soto und Julia Natividad Rodriguez Suárez, denen die erneute Inhaftierung drohte. Sie waren in der Vergangenheit rechtswidrig wegen angeblicher „terroristischer Straftaten" angeklagt worden. Noch im selben Monat hob der Oberste Gerichtshof des Landes die Haftbefehle gegen beide auf, so dass sie nicht mehr in Gefahr waren, inhaftiert zu werden. Die peruanische Menschenrechtsorganisation „Asociación Ministerio Diaconal Paz y Esperanza", die sich ebenfalls für die Häftlinge eingesetzt hatte, teilte amnesty international in einem Brief mit: „Wir gehen davon aus, dass die von Ihnen veröffentlichte Eilaktion in dem Fall eine wichtige Rolle gespielt hat. Dank der Urgent Action sind zwei Unschuldige, die in einem unfairen Verfahren der Mitgliedschaft in einer bewaffneten Oppositionsgruppe bezichtigt wurden, in Freiheit und bei ihren Familien sind, während das Gericht ihre Fälle überprüft". (UA 116/06)

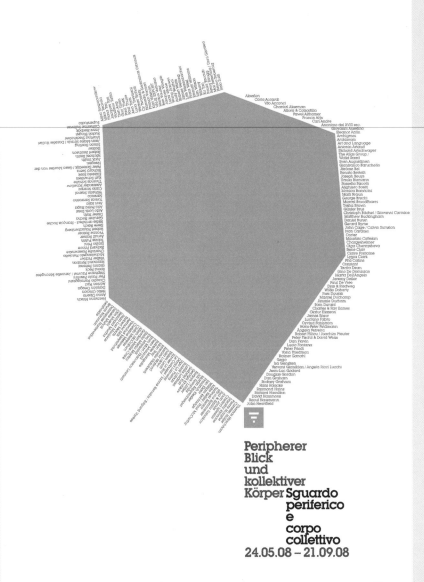

This design by Tomato incorporates hierarchy, distinguishing sections of information, and experiments with balance and white space.

Chapter 3 : Designing with type

This chapter discusses the various issues raised when designing with type. It will look at the design process, for both print- and screen-based work, from ideas generation and design considerations to artwork and preproduction. It will explore the techniques available (traditional and digital), tools, design issues in relation to various products, and situations where type forms an integral part of a design. It will look at examples of experimentation and risk-taking in the context of the design.

There are various stages to design, including research and analysis, ideas development, evaluation, and production. This implies that the process has to be linear and logical. However, an individual chooses how to work; it may be methodically, but is just as likely to be spontaneously and messily. It is when you need to communicate with others about your design that logical development may be necessary to help them understand where you are going with it.

The design process

Type and letterforms feature in most visual communication design. Many of the processes related to this discipline, for example concept and ideas generation, sketchbook and development work, reflection, evaluation, and production planning, will be similar for different applications. An important aspect of all design work is experimentation with materials, techniques, and processes. There may be certain differences in approach depending on the product to be designed, so, for example, type design for packaging might be tackled somewhat differently from that for a website, as the way people view and consume each product varies.

Whatever the final product, when confronted with a design brief, project, or problem many of us will form initial responses in our minds before committing anything to paper or screen. It is important to record those first ideas as spontaneously as possible before going on to more formal concept generation.

A playful and decorative design by Hannah Rummery uses a fusion of traditional and modern styles of typeface for this innovative tourist information poster where the type forms the outline of Wales.

Ferran Valverde Garcia has chosen a
traditional typeface, Garamond Italic, for
this editorial design foldout.

Ideas generation

Ideas can come from anywhere, but influences can be roughly divided into two categories: those that stem from your own preferences, experiences, and personality and those that derive from external sources, such as fashion, trends, and historical examples. Inspiration can be triggered by research on what has gone before or what others are doing, experiments with various aspects of the design, and brainstorming.

Most people absorb visual stimuli without realizing it, which can be dangerous if you end up unwittingly reproducing an existing design. There are many examples of this, and some cases even get as far as legal actions for infringement of intellectual copyright. However, a lot of design borrows from the past and being influenced by something is not the same as copying it: a fusion of different historical and cultural references can be a good starting point for innovative design. It is normal to be affected by contemporary trends, but innovative work usually breaks away from what is currently fashionable and makes its own mark.

When looking at others' work, try to identify what has been successful and what hasn't. A good area to focus on is the choice of typeface: many typefaces that were originally designed in the 17th and 18th centuries, such as Caslon and Garamond, are tried and tested and still used today. Classics of the 20th century include Frutiger and Helvetica.

When recording ideas, put down everything you think of, even if it comes to mind when you haven't got a notebook with you: make a note on your phone, scrap of paper, beer mat—anything that comes to hand. You don't want to miss landing the big one—the idea that's better than all the

As these thumbnail sketches by Sherrie Thai of Shaire Productions illustrate, it is more important to record your ideas quickly before they evaporate than to produce carefully crafted artworks.

This is a good example of a page from a sketchbook collection of type ephemera.

others. We often forget ideas that come to us at difficult times: you say to yourself, "I'll put that one down in the morning," but it rarely happens. The enemy of creativity is self-censorship—no idea is too stupid or obvious to ignore. It's better to have too many ideas and have to sift through them than to struggle with too few. These records of ideas are a valuable resource, which can be revisited for other projects or just browsed through as a reminder of your creative abilities when you experience writer's block or blank-page panic.

The way you record ideas is up to you, but if you need to explain them to someone, such as a client or a tutor, small, quick sketches (thumbnails) are a useful tool. Remember that you will need to translate these to a larger scale to realize the design, which means that the format, i.e. whether it is to be landscape or portrait, needs to be considered at this stage.

This series of webpages by Petra Sell demonstrates continuity—although the kind of information on the right-hand side is different on each page, the overall feel is similar. This is brought about through consistent layout, typeface, color, and size of type.

As we are primarily concerned with type and lettering, make sure that you have an idea of how typefaces perform (remembering that the same typeface may work differently in print and on screen). As suggested in chapter 2, it is worth recording experiments with different typefaces, but introduce other factors such as family variations, scale, color, texture, etc. Collect samples of type—these may be physical artifacts, such as plastic lettering or Letraset, photographs, ephemera, pictures from magazines, snippets of type, and so on.

Creativity within a house style

Sometimes, particularly when working on magazines or newspapers, you are more likely to design a section or double-page spread within an existing publication than to create something completely from scratch. This will mean that your design is constrained by the defined style of that publication. For example, the typeface for body text may be predetermined. However, there may be more flexibility in the choice of typeface for other aspects of the design, such as title and pull quotes. This allows the designer some scope to reinforce the communication through choice of typeface, an aspect of the use of type and lettering that is covered in more depth in chapter 4. When recurring aspects of a design, such as body text typeface, have been chosen, you can set up style sheets or templates that act as the basis for each page, which may then be customized for different articles and sections of the publication. When setting up style sheets or templates, you can also define where and how columns of text link to each other. Text may run throughout the publication, in sections, or just in a couple of columns on a page: this is referred to as text linking, flowing, or threading.

TOWARDS AN ACCOUNTABLE CAPITALISM

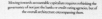

Moving towards accountable capitalism requires rethinking the governance of not just the banks or credit rating agencies, but of the overall architecture encompassing them.

People tend to evaluate evidence in a selective fashion when they have a stake in reaching a particular conclusion or outcome.

SEE NO EVIL: WHY WE OVERLOOK OTHER PEOPLE'S UNETHICAL BEHAVIOUR

We care deeply about what others think of us and, as a result, 'mattering maps' exert a powerful influence on our behaviour.

How Mattering Maps Affect Behaviour

New Challenges For Corporate Governance

Just as a re-balancing of the director's role was taking shape post-Sarbanes-Oxley, expected reforms in the areas of risk management and compensation will once again challenge director effectiveness.

In these double-page spreads for *Rotman* magazine, Brian Banton and Clea Forkert demonstrate the variety that can be achieved within a predetermined style.

Todd Moy of Viget Labs has produced detailed working drawings for the design and coding of a website.

Luis Mendo has used color-coding on this flatplan to identify the various categories of spread within the publication he is designing.

Working ideas up

Once you have homed in on an idea, there are various methods of working through how the design will be realized. Much depends on the application you are working within. For example, flatplans are used for editorial design, storyboards for animation, graphic novels, etc., flowcharts for websites and multimedia artifacts, dummies for book covers, and maquettes for packaging and point-of-purchase materials. Such templates help the designer to visualize even the most adventurous concepts. They may also be useful for testing practical considerations such as visibility, stackability, and constructability.

TIP

During the design process, it is useful to step back and reflect on your work in progress. Walking away from the work for a while helps you to see it with fresh eyes. There are many techniques to help you see your work as others might see it, such as squinting at it, looking at it in a mirror, or, if it is on screen, flipping it vertically or horizontally (if the program you are using has this facility).

When working ideas up from thumbnails or flatplans to full-size prototypes, it is important to ensure that the typeface(s) used will work in that context. Type may look fine at the thumbnail stage but when taken to full size can look entirely different. Try a range of typefaces in different sizes, combinations, colors, etc. Don't be afraid to experiment. Many typographers will say that putting serifs with serifs and sans serifs with sans serifs is not a good idea because the two typefaces will not provide enough contrast and will tend to cancel each other out, but try it and see what happens.

Fluid Studio have used a mix of typefaces to produce this poster.

Using a short word that includes at least one ascender and one descender (e.g. "lazy," "paddle," "quick"), experiment with producing the word in a variety of typefaces, sizes, weights, widths, and styles. Try serif and sans serif typefaces as well as display and ornamental fonts. Keep a note of which typefaces are which, in case you want to refer to them again. When you have gathered several different typographic versions of your word, put them in pairs to see how they work in combination with each other. For example, match a serif with a sans serif, an ornamental with a simple sans serif.

This activity may be carried out on screen or by tracing letterforms. Alternatively, you can look for examples of different typefaces in magazines or on websites, but, if you do this, you may not find enough examples of the same word, so you may need to use different words to compare typefaces.

top: A student has experimented with several different typefaces to get a feel for the variety available.

above: In the upper part of this example, a student has experimented with typefaces by putting them together in random pairs. In the lower part, she has made more studied pairings, considering such factors as contrast or similarity in tone, weight, x-height, and shape.

above: This student has collected versions of the same word in different typefaces and sizes. She has pasted them together in different categories and started to label some of the typefaces.

Experimentation

The larger the range of experiments you make with
type and lettering, the more you will come to understand
the differences between typefaces, their strengths, and
limitations. You will also become familiar with how
a typeface performs in different settings, at different
weights and widths, sizes and colors, and how it reacts
with other typefaces and other elements such as images,
symbols, and rules. As part of this process, you will
develop your own preferences and get to know which
typefaces work best for which circumstances and how
they sit within the design.

 **Pitfall: Experimentation does not necessarily
mean throwing stuff around; it may be quite
systematic and controlled—it depends on
your method of working.**

The other aspect of experimentation is the use of a variety
of different techniques, materials, and media. If you are
designing for screen, try to develop your ideas using the
technology rather than letting the technology define your
ideas. Come up with an idea that may not be practical and
then try to find a way of realizing it, which may lead along
other interesting avenues, rather than being limited by
what the software instructions tell you is possible.

Brasilia Prima have used a combination of
typefaces that complement the images to
give a retro feel to this poster design.

above: In this double-page spread Li Mei Tan has taken a creative approach, but it is clear that he understands balance and other typographic principles such as readability.

below: Fluid Design have chosen an unusual combination of typefaces for this visually strong website design.

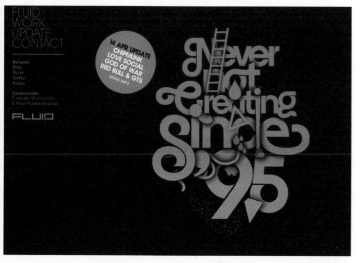

The rules and breaking the rules

Although experimentation is important in developing a creative approach to design, it is useful to have a good understanding of the principles behind good typography and design because adventurous work often develops from a sound knowledge of typographic conventions.

We've already discussed issues such as legibility, readability, symmetry, text color, choice of typeface, background, texture of stock, screen resolution, white space, and alignment. There are many other considerations, such as the need to take into account the more fluid nature of design for screen where text and images may be added, subtracted, or altered in some way postproduction. This flexibility may become an essential part of your design—for example, you may leave virtual space for additions.

Design considerations

Other issues that could have a strong impact on your design include hierarchy, emphasis, contrast, bleed, and text runaround. These need to be considered early on in the design and in relation to the content of the text and the interpretation you are trying to achieve. You would not want to make a serious article look too light or humorous, or vice versa.

Hierarchy

If you analyze the way the information has been structured in this book, you will see that there is a hierarchy common to all chapters. This consists of chapter title, headings, subheads, captions, and tips and other ancillaries. In this publication, the hierarchy is standardized throughout the chapters, but sometimes a flexible hierarchy can be established. This is useful in magazine, brochure, and Web design where there is a need to have consistency but also variety to maintain the viewer's interest. As long as the reader can follow what's happening, hierarchical systems may be unconventional—for example, placing a title part way down a block of text rather than at the top.

Establishing hierarchy will not necessarily mean that the most important piece of information (usually the title) is the biggest or boldest. As with all aspects of design, you can approach this creatively and experiment with using, for example, a smaller and perhaps different typeface or a lighter/different color for the title in a way that draws attention to it.

Robert Ferrell has used a serif typeface in a simple single-column layout for this piece of work based on soldiers' experiences of war.

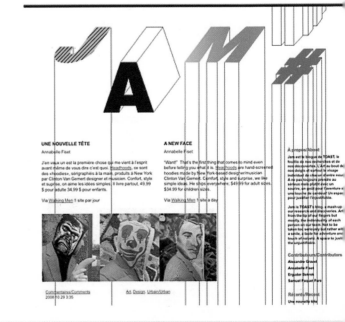

right: Annabelle Fiset has used a combination of drawn letterforms, type, and images for this webpage, which has a lively context.

opposite: There is a simple hierarchy, with the most important information at the base of the layout, in this poster design by Kim.

Janez Strnad

POBIČ, ki je v svojo domačo učiteljico
vrgel stol in s tem dosegel, da se ni več vrnila.
TRINAJSTLETNIK, ki je med počitnicami
predelal gimnazijske učbenike za
matematiko in zasovražil maturo.
ROMANTIČNA LJUBEZEN, ki se je sprevrgla
v dramo. *Einstein zasebno.*
MIROVNIK, ki je v gandhijevski maniri
pozival svet, naj se upre z vojaško
nepokorščino in odvrže orožje.
FIZIK, ki je spremenil tok znanosti.
AVTOR »najslavnejše enačbe vseh časov«,
ki je zbudila radovednost ljudi po vsem
svetu, ne da bi jo razumeli. *Einstein javno.*

9 789612 410339

Janez Strnad

Einstein

Zakaj me nihče
ne razume
in me imajo
vsi radi?

SLOVENSKI FIZIK dr. Janez Strnad, ki je
o delu Alberta Einsteina napisal številne
strokovne in poljudne prispevke, se je v knjigi
*Einstein: Zakaj me nihče ne razume in me imajo
vsi radi?* posvetil njegovemu življenju.
Podobo slavnega znanstvenika gradi
z razvojem dogodkov, stališč in odnosov
do najbližjih, kot jih razkrivajo Einsteinovi
zapisi, pisma in odkritja njegovih biografov.
Pri tem ne obide fizikovih zasebnih in
družbenih dilem, s katerimi se je soočal.
Umeščene v zgodovinski kontekst bralcu
ponujajo možnost, da sam poišče odgovor
na Einsteinovo (samo)spraševanje: »Zakaj me
nihče ne razume in me imajo vsi radi?«
Strnadova monografija o Albertu Einsteinu je
izšla v dveh knjigah. Druga, *Einstein: E=mc²*,
analizira Einsteinovo delo v fiziki.

Modrijan

4900 SIT

Janez Strnad

Zakaj me nihče ne razume in me imajo vsi radi?

Tomato Košir has used a larger type size,
different color, and heavier typeface for
emphasis in this design.

right: This double-page spread designed by Moa Nordahl uses contrast in a wide variety of ways. The title has been split between patterned and plain text, the column measure varies, and there are different weights and sizes of text—all of which provides interest through contrast. Also, the patterned background of the left-hand page contrasts strongly with the white space on the right-hand page.

below: Brent Barson's "F is for Fail" multimedia project demonstrates contrast in a series of words associated with the letters of the alphabet. For the letter "Q," he juxtaposes different sizes of type, colors, typefaces, and still and moving type.

Emphasis

One of the ways to define a hierarchy of heading levels is through emphasis—using different styles of type to signal different levels of heading. A simple example would be a bold title, italic subhead, and standard body text. However, emphasis can also be used to introduce hierarchy within the body text. It is often used to draw attention to a particular word or phrase by *highlighting* it in some way: often in *italic* or **bold** versions of the typeface.

Contrast

Contrast can also help to establish hierarchy, as well as making the design more interesting and exciting. Contrast may be achieved in various ways: between typefaces (the most obvious being serif vs. sans serif); between large and small type or hand-rendered and mass-produced type; between different colors, tones, textures, weights, or densities of type. All of these techniques, and many others, will establish the tone of a design and enable you to guide the viewer.

Bleed and runaround

Bleed is the term used to describe when a layout element, usually an image, runs off the edge of a page or screen. It is not used as much with text, but it is a useful trick to help the page seem bigger than it is or to give the impression that there is more to the page than meets the eye.

Text may also be wrapped around an image or other object, which may give the design a more fluid appearance. Known as text wrap or runaround, this device can also be used to draw attention to key information or to relate type to an image by copying its shape. To maximize its impact, runaround should be carefully considered and not overused. This need for restraint applies to many aspects of design that can now be implemented in design software at the click of a mouse.

Pitfall: When wrapping text around an object, don't rely on the default settings—take the time to consider the distance between the text and the object as well as its relationship to column width and other elements of the design.

In this double-page spread Attak have used text runaround to emphasize the curved shapes in the images and give cohesion to the design.

design@Typographic use text runaround to give this Web design a dynamic feel.

This powerful double-page spread by Roman Krikheli bleeds type into the gutter and off the top of the page to emphasize the diagonal composition, but the type has been carefully positioned to ensure that it is still legible.

above: Aleksander Blücher has distorted the letterforms to draw the reader toward the body text.

below: Jiansheng Cui has combined type on a curve with type radiating from the circle to give a dynamic feel to this complex design.

Manipulating text

Many software programs provide facilities to, for example, distort, skew, stretch, or reverse/mirror text, or to bend it on a curve or other shape. As with runarounds, these forms of text manipulation require care and fine-tuning both in execution and in consideration of the context of the overall design.

When stretching text, or manipulating it in any way, look at the structure of the typeface and ask a few questions. Does it need altering? Why was it designed in this form? Could it be that the designer has spent a long time getting it right in terms of its shape, balance, proportions, etc., and that you are just tinkering with something that works well as it is? Would it be better to look at alternative typefaces or members of the type family? Will distortion add to the design? What message are you trying to convey by making a distortion? Will the type be readable/legible? Does the type need to be readable/legible?

Manipulating type can enhance a design and help with communication. A good example is running type onto a curve for the design of a badge, CD, or other circular product where the format constrains the design.

Software packages feature all sorts of tricks and tools for altering type—but just because they are there doesn't mean you have to use them. Having said this, just like more traditional tools, they are interesting to explore, as long as you think carefully about why you are using them.

 Pitfall: When setting type on a curve or circle, remember to adjust the spaces between letterforms and take care that vertical lines do not crash into each other.

right: This website by Sudar Pitarevic, although digital by necessity, has a hand-produced appearance. It uses a range of textures and shapes to produce a visually exciting splash page.

above: You can achieve some great effects using old wooden type found in a flea market, thrift store, or swap meet and an ordinary ink stamp pad.

right: This design by Abel Martínez Foronda incorporates digital type and type that has been digitally constructed or altered to form strong shapes and images.

far right: In this poster designed by Fons Hickmann the type has been manipulated so that it appears to be entering from the right-hand side.

Tools

There are many different tools available to use in designing with or creating letterforms, ranging from traditional letterpress and word-processed type to the handmade. You may also decide to use a combination of any or many of these.

If you want to use traditional letterpress, you will either have to source a printer who can provide this specialist service (and probably pay for it) or you could acquire some metal or wooden type and experiment with it yourself (see opposite left).

Computer-generated type may range from something very simple created using a word-processing program to an individually designed letterform produced in a specialist package such as Adobe Illustrator.

Programs such as Adobe Illustrator are also used by many designers to manipulate or adjust existing letterforms. Good examples of this may be found in logo design and illustrated capital letters. If you decide to manipulate an existing typeface, it is worth remembering that many commercial typefaces are copyrighted and therefore you will need to check with the designer before publishing your adaptation.

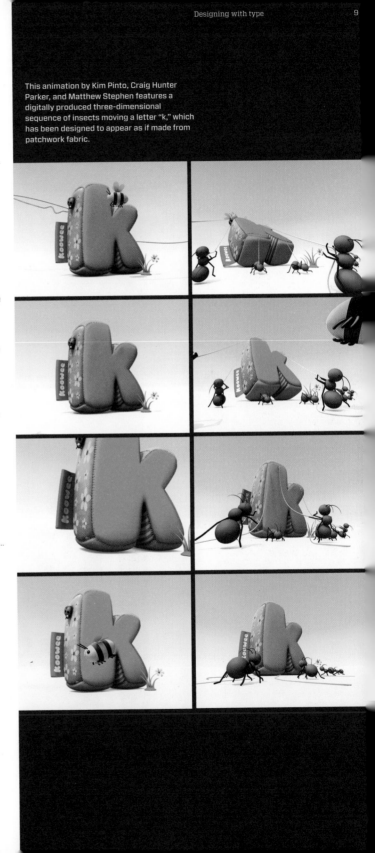

This animation by Kim Pinto, Craig Hunter Parker, and Matthew Stephen features a digitally produced three-dimensional sequence of insects moving a letter "k," which has been designed to appear as if made from patchwork fabric.

Experiment with creating individual letterforms using a variety of materials in order to understand the different shapes and effects produced by different media and techniques. These may range from vegetable matter to steel and glass and may be produced at different scales depending on the materials and then photographed for use in print or on screen.

At the simplest level, a letterform may be created by hand using pencils, paint, or potatoes (see page 57). You may also consider more sophisticated methods such as silkscreen or linoprint. The resulting letterforms may be digitally photographed or scanned and manipulated by, for example, adding texture, changing or adding colors, altering scale, distressing, and distorting.

This logo design by Luxury of Protest is a good example of manipulated type.

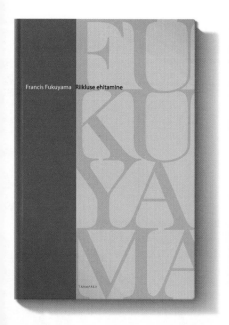

Dan Mikkin, at the Estonian design agency The Brand Manual, adopts two completely different approaches to these book covers. The first design, using digital type, is clean and formal; the second, featuring hand-drawn type for the title and digital type just for the author's name, is far more textural.

Paul Hollingworth has created this dynamic logo for a band and produced it in wood and Plexiglas. Once physical letterforms have been created, they can be adapted in all kinds of ways—for example, by adding an illumination effect, as in this case.

Refining

Having generated and developed ideas, experimented, tested, and worked ideas up to full size, you need to refine the design before preparing for production.

This is the stage where it is good to walk away from the design for a while in order to return to it afresh. It is important to look out for problems and inconsistencies before finalizing for production. This process might include, for example: ensuring that the images relate to the text they are closest to; assessing how the body text balances with any images used; and checking consistency of typefaces, style, etc. Stylistic inconsistencies can occur if text is pasted in at a late stage. You may also need to check spellings in titles and subheadings (usually the body text will be the responsibility of the proofreader).

TIP Make sure that you have a dated signature to certify that the text has been proofread and approved—this is called signing off.

This part of the design process is also your last opportunity, before production planning, to reflect on what you have done and check for fine detail such as widows and orphans, hyphenation, and awkward/dislocated text linking.

Mozambique Toy Soldier Typography

by Happy Centro, Italy

Happy Centro produced this type for a poster for the *Imagining Mozambique* exhibition, a showcase for thought-provoking art bringing attention to the day-to-day life of the children of Mozambique.

The designer, Federico Galvani, did not initially know a lot about the issues in Mozambique, so the first thing he did was to turn to the internet. He found it interesting that such a superficial approach can sometimes suggest creative avenues to explore. He discovered that the country experienced civil war between 1977 and 1992. This information resonated with the designer, who was born in 1977 and therefore would have been a child at the same time as children in Mozambique were experiencing a bloody conflict. The thought that these children had not been able to enjoy childhood games sparked off the idea of war as a game, which inspired Galvani to use toy soldiers as a visual metaphor.

Designed by Federico Galvani; photographed by Federico Padovani; with the support of Jamie N Kim, Mo Manager, and Wieden+KennedyWork.

Working within his paper template, the designer constructs three-dimensional letterforms from toy soldiers using a glue gun.

Once constructed, the letterforms are colored in the green, black, yellow, and red of the Mozambique flag.

Galvani has attached wire letterforms to the larger constructions made from toy soldiers and cars.

Mozambique, officially the Republic of Mozambique (Portuguese: Moçambique or República de Moçambique), is a country in southeastern Africa bordered by the Indian Ocean to the east, Tanzania to the north, Malawi and Zambia to the northwest, Zimbabwe to the west and Swaziland and South Africa to the southwest. It was explored by Vasco da Gama in 1498 and colonized by Portugal in 1505. By 1510, the Portuguese had virtual control of all of the former Swahili sultanates on the east African coast. From about 1500, Portuguese trading posts and forts became regular ports of call on the new route to the east. Mozambique became independent in 1975, to which it became the People's Republic of Mozambique shortly after, and **was the scene of an intense civil war from 1977 to 1992**. The country is a member of the Community of Portuguese Language Countries and the Commonwealth of Nations and an observer of the Francophonie. Mozambique (Moçambique) was named by the Portuguese after Msumbiji, the Swahili name of Mozambique Island and port-town. Mozambique's life expectancy and infant mortality rates are both among the worst ranked in the world. Its Human Development Index is one of the lowest on earth.

Wikipedia — The Free Encyclopedia
Federico Galvani — Happycentro — Italy — 2009

Photography by Federico Padovani

Craig Redman's simple but effective use of
type as image clearly reinforces the message.

Chapter 4 : Communication

This chapter is concerned with how the designer can control type to convey a certain message, emotion, or idea. It will explore the meanings that can be communicated through variables such as appropriate or inappropriate typefaces, balance and imbalance, harmony and discord, symmetry and asymmetry. It discusses how to make a type design suitable for its likely audience, taking into consideration differences in scale and context, for example, between a poster and a design for a touch-screen icon. Also covered is the potential for subversive approaches, such as creating edginess by inappropriate use of everyday type or objects or deliberate flouting of conventions.

Forms of communication

Type is found in most areas of visual communication and falls into two main categories: persuasion (rhetoric) and information (non-rhetoric). Persuasion includes areas of advertising, such as posters, websites, TV advertisements, and packaging. Information relates to most editorial matter, such as magazines, books, newspapers, comics, information booklets, and brochures. Many of these genres have completely different functions: an instruction booklet, for example, needs to provide clear explanation, whereas an advertisement has to attract attention and create a perception of the product being promoted. The use of type in each case will differ accordingly.

Even predominantly image- or sound-based media need interpretation through use of type in order to ensure accessibility. This includes subtitling for foreign languages and for the deaf and hard of hearing.

The boundaries between information- and persuasion-based type can be blurred. Some websites, for example, are purely advertising-based and others are information-based, but most fall somewhere in between and combine aspects of both.

Whichever area, or combination of areas, of visual communication you are working in, your type design should engage the reader with the message. You will need to consider how you direct your audience to the message, help them navigate around the message, and guide them to an understanding of the overall meaning of the communication.

Unlike images, which communicate quickly and directly, type delivers its meaning invisibly and subtly: the viewer is not conscious of the process. This is linked to readability issues that we discussed in chapter 2. Persuasion is considered all the more powerful when people are unaware of it. There are many factors involved in this subliminal process, such as choice of typeface, and style, color, and weight of type, but one of the most important is the use of hierarchy. This helps to draw readers in and enables you to deliver the message and aid interpretation of meaning by guiding them around the information.

above: KentLyons have taken an innovative approach to persuading people to use their local library.

below: Studio Oscar fitted text to the outline of an image to reinforce the message about homelessness.

THINNING
NUMBERS

WE WERE NINETY-SIX WHEN WE ARRIVED, WE, THE ITALIANS OF CONVOY 174,000; ONLY TWENTY-NINE OF US SURVIVED UNTIL OCTOBER, AND OF THESE, EIGHT WENT IN THE LAST SELECTION. WE ARE NOW TWENTY-ONE AND THE WINTER HAS HARDLY BEGUN. HOW MANY OF US WILL BE ALIVE AT THE NEW YEAR? HOW MANY WHEN SPRING BEGINS?

PRIMO LEVI, IF THIS IS A MAN

Meanings

Choice of typeface is one of the most fundamental factors in conveying the meaning of a type design. We have seen how a classic typeface works well for a serious publication and a sans serif, modern typeface can indicate a lighter touch (see page 27). An article on period furniture in a lifestyle magazine may call for a retro typeface, whereas a children's story will probably require something more dynamic. In the latter context, a calligraphic typeface might convey the desired qualities of spontaneity and immediacy, as well as giving a hand-produced look, but it could also leave the overall impression of something unfinished, too casual, or frivolous. This is another time when you need to step back and evaluate your work before making final decisions.

TIP Key to helping people interpret meaning is having an understanding of it yourself. Ideally you should read the text you are designing, but at the very least you should have a clear idea of the content. Often editors will provide a synopsis or outline of content if you are working on a book or other lengthy editorial matter, so you may not have to read the whole text.

Symmetry and asymmetry, and the closely related balance and imbalance, can also be exploited to communicate meaning. A symmetrical design, where both sides are similar, will tend to give a formal feel to a layout, whereas an asymmetrical design could suggest a lighter ambience. A symmetrical layout will always be balanced: if you drew a line down the middle, the right side would mirror the left. An asymmetrical design may also appear balanced if the various components are evenly, though irregularly, distributed across the layout, but it will look unbalanced if, for example, there is a large area of type on the right side and only a small image to the top or bottom left of the layout. A balanced design can be interpreted as calm, stable, structured, and formal, whereas an unbalanced design will usually make the viewer feel slightly edgy and uncomfortable; it might also give an active, informal feel to the design. Although symmetrical in form, centered type can share the lively, energetic qualities of an asymmetrical design. This is linked to the readability issues discussed in

178
Sensaway typeface in developement
infinite contrast is the thing
© Aron Jancso, 2009

This design by Áron Jancsó achieves a fine balance in an asymmetrical layout.

right: Dimitris Kanellopoulos has used asymmetry in this poster to give it an edgy feel.

below: The balanced, symmetrical layout of this movie poster by Unusual Design Group contrasts with the playing-card metaphor and the dollar and revolver icons. This opposition suggests a game of high stakes taking place beneath a calm surface.

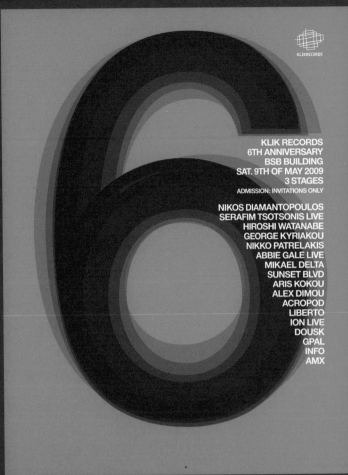

Peter Kowalski of Wordboner.com cleverly combines two different, but related words by overlaying colored type. This makes the design difficult to read, playing a visual game with the viewer to reinforce the message.

chapter 2; centered type is not that easy to read and this can cause visual disturbance.

Often, designs will incorporate multiple meanings that work on many levels. Some may be obvious, but others could be hidden or complex, underpinning messages intended to reach the audience subliminally. An example would be the use of particular imagery and type to generate a feeling of fear or insecurity in propaganda or a feeling of warmth and familiarity in advertising.

The relationship between a typeface and its meaning may be obvious—for example, using a handmade style of typeface in a brochure for a craft fair—or it may be more subtle. For example, traditional serif typefaces such as Bembo derive from handwriting, so choosing such a typeface for an autobiography would reinforce the personal nature of the text.

Harmony and contrast may be incorporated in designs to help convey meaning. Harmonious typefaces, such as those belonging to the same family, can deliver a message of comfort and familiarity, whereas discordant typefaces, such as two different but similar sans serifs, can make a design feel unsettling. Similarly, a static arrangement will make a design feel stable and sensible, whereas a design that has plenty of movement will appear active and exciting.

Another way of creating harmony or contrast is through the relationship between text and image. For example, an image

This poster by Hassan Haider achieves a harmonious feel with its subtle use of type.

PIČULIN
HRAST
BᴲLIN
LAZAR
ⴹIDᴧN
PATUOKAR

above: Faced with an influx of new homeowners from across Europe, the Slovenian village of Ciginj conducted a project to research and preserve traditional house names. On this poster design for the project, TipoBrda have chosen a suitably conservative serif typeface.

right: This typeface has been designed by Ale Paul to look as if it has been hand written, which would make it a good choice to communicate a sense of friendship or informality.

Š SUDTIPOS NEW RELEASES
MAY 2011

Amor

Wild & windy

Southern

Cooking Ingredients

Quick times in a fast culture

New Orleans

Ligatures addition

Spiced Herbs

Viento

WWW.SUDTIPOS.COM

insound
sxsw party

liars
vivian girls
surfer blood
delorean
small black

----

thursday, march 18
12-6pm

club deville
900 red river road, austin

21+, free entry
$3 beer bracelet

presented by
saucony originals

top: This design by Magma makes use of both closure and text bleed to focus the reader's attention on the quotation. By forcing us to work harder than normal to decipher the text, the design slows us down and makes us think about the content.

above: In this double-page spread Harry Seifert uses contrasting typefaces to indicate not just two different voices but two different languages.

of an elephant would contrast with a section of text about nanotechnology but be in harmony with an article about wildlife. Similarly, typefaces themselves can provide contrast—for example, a soft, delicate script typeface for a text about the dangers of ignoring crime. The comforting typeface might be used to set up a sense of complacency in the reader that would be undermined by the theme of the text.

Good use of type, particularly in terms of hierarchy, can even help in clarifying difficult-to-understand texts or concepts. An example of this would be a complex form, such as a tax return, which can daunt and confuse many people. A clear, easily read typeface together with well-organized layering of information and signposting can make all the difference.

Meaning may be enhanced by the use of the techniques of closure and bleed. Closure is accomplished by capitalizing on the tendency for the human brain to complete partial forms, such as making a "C" into an "O." Bleed is a mechanism for extending the boundaries of a section or page (see page 88). You will often find this used in print design where images are bled off the edge of the page but it is also a good way of using missing type or sections of type to extend the page visually. It is also useful to indicate the feeling that there is more there than is obvious, like making something appear bigger than it actually is.

Comparison may be used as a way of enhancing meaning. We have talked about experimenting with different combinations of typefaces, scales, and weights in chapter 3, and these may help to convey a message. A good example of this is the use of two distinctly different typefaces, perhaps Fette Fraktur (a heavy, Germanic typeface of the sort found in early manuscripts) with Frutiger (a spacious, light sans serif typeface), to indicate two opposing points of view.

There are many different approaches to interpreting a feel or style in order to convey meaning so that the content or context of a communication is understood more easily. To help you develop your own methods, you should analyze the effectiveness of others' attempts as well as trying your own experiments. You will learn an enormous amount from others' successes (and failures) as well as your own.

About
Work
Contact

Robin Uleman specialises in: editorial design that requires a distinctive character and identity work for people and organisations that have a story to tell. The aim is to translate strategic objectives into meaningful design solutions by creating a visual language that communicates in an authentic and intelligent way.

Works and has worked with: Ahrend, Bert Bakker, The Beach, B.V. Associatief, Cultuurfabriek, Dietwee, Frame Publishers, KesselsKramer, NAi, NEOW Business & Brand, Meulenhoff, Atelier Satyendra Pakhalé, Premsela / Dutch Platform for Design and Fashion, School, THEY, Veenman Publishers and Henk Wildschut Photography.

robinuleman

Robin Uleman's website design is clean and simple, leaving space around information.

Context

Designers with strong identities are often chosen for projects that fit within their personal style. Whether this is the case or not, the context should be the first consideration in terms of style and feel to ensure effective communication. Certain contexts are strongly associated with a particular style. For example, science-fiction book covers often feature sans serif or modern-looking display typefaces. When designing for a context that has a distinctive style, ask yourself whether you intend to be faithful to the style or whether you intend to subvert it by experimenting with alternatives. Conversely, if you are designing a product for a wide audience, for example, a general-fiction book cover, be careful about using a style closely associated with a subgenre, because the specific cues may not resonate with anyone who is not familiar with them. You can quote from styles and genres to good effect as a way of communicating ideas in the form of pastiche, much as Roy Lichtenstein uses comic-book lettering in his paintings to evoke the popular culture associated with pulp fiction and the comic.

Not all designs are one-offs; there are many occasions when a design is produced as a multiple or as a series—an example being a print or Web magazine. If this is the case, it is important to retain the style and continuity but ensure that each iteration has its own identity or flavor.

Whatever style is adopted, there are advantages in avoiding fussy, complicated approaches and keeping things as simple as possible. There is an increasing amount of visual, verbal, and written noise in our lives; it is useful sometimes to cut through the interference with a clear, straightforward solution. Neutrality is another way of achieving this effect: choosing a bland, familiar typeface, such as Arial, can make a message speak for itself, without encouraging inference or partiality.

Select two books from contrasting genres, such as crime thriller and chick lit. Produce two book covers for each book, one in the accepted style and one in the style of the other genre. To carry out this activity, you will need to research the sort of typography that usually features on book covers in your two chosen genres.

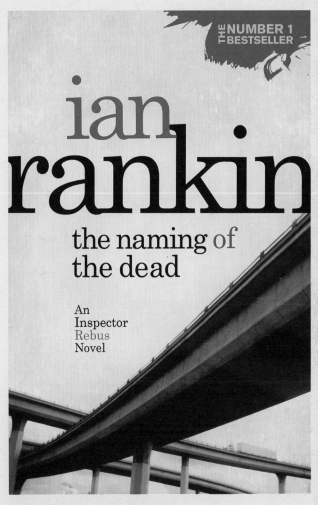

These two designs by Cabin demonstrate the use of type style appropriate to the content: the crime novel uses a sober, uncompromising serif typeface, whereas the chick lit book's title is in hand-drawn lettering that suggests warmth and "kookiness."

AKADEMIA TAŃCA

passion
engagement
love
pain
tears
blood
heart

★ TALENT / PASJA / EKSPRESJA

left: Michal Bialogrzywy has taken the concept of a splash page literally for this Dance Academy website.

above: The strong contrast in scale between the letter "g" and the rest of the type in this design by Áron Jancsó immediately draws the viewer's eye.

left: When designing for an audience on the move, clarity is normally paramount. However, in this series of posters Huda Abdul Aziz uses cropped letterforms to create a sense of intrigue as travelers walk along the station concourse.

Great, Britain.

We're flying low cost to Asia.

from £179

Impact

Any design that stands out from its rivals in some way will have an impact. Sometimes, as we have seen, even a bland, neutral design can provide impact if the audience has become jaded by more lively designs that jostle for attention. The use of an incongruous typeface can make a design memorable. An element of surprise may also be achieved by use of type in an unusual or uncomfortable style, size, positioning, or color.

There are many other ways of providing impact, such as contrast in scale (for example, a small capital letter beginning a long lowercase word). Other methods include isolating a small section of type from the rest of the text, drastic cropping of letterforms, interrupting the rhythm of a sentence or passage of text, and choosing unusual or discordant typefaces that cause the reader/viewer to pause.

Impact may be used dramatically in website design, where a splash or opening page will be designed to invite you into the site rather than bounce off elsewhere. People need little excuse to navigate away from websites, whereas the turning of the pages of a physical book or magazine creates a natural flow, so the creation of impact is arguably even more important in Web design than in print.

Posters lining an escalator shaft are read when the audience is moving. The type, therefore, needs to be easy to read for an audience with little time to absorb information, and able to create an impact to attract attention in the first place. The audience needs to be able to interpret the message, which may in itself provide the shock, quickly and efficiently. It is important to know, if possible, the context in which a design is to be situated so that you have an idea of what it will be competing against. For example, if you are designing a poster that is going to end up on a bulletin board vying for attention with lots of other, well-designed posters, what can you do to make yours stand out?

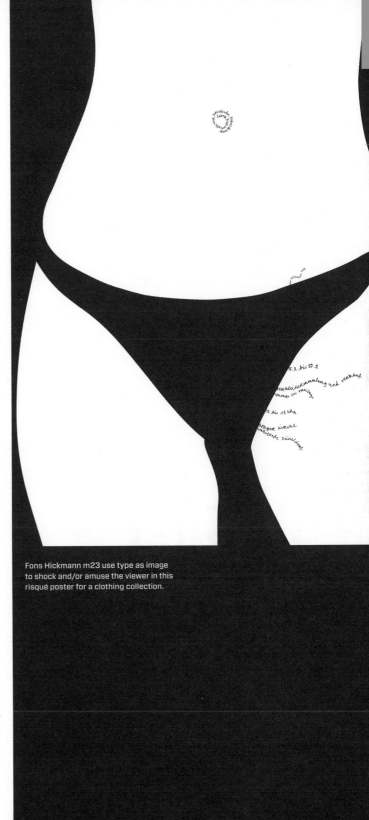

Fons Hickmann m23 use type as image to shock and/or amuse the viewer in this risqué poster for a clothing collection.

Rishi Sodha uses repetition to imprint the phrase "Tibetan supermarket" in the minds of the audience.

Rhythm and repetition

Rhythm and repetition are important ways of establishing continuity in a design, which helps to ensure the message is conveyed. It is natural for people to tune in to visual rhythm or repetition in the same way that they respond to poetry or music.

In design terms, repetition is the direct replication of a certain word, phrase, or motif, perhaps with a different typographic treatment, and so is usually easy to spot. Rhythm tends to be less obvious; it may occur at the structural level of the design—for example, in the use of hierarchy—rather than in individual components.

Because rhythm is subtler, there is less danger of it being overused. Repetition, however, can become, well, repetitive. For example, if you were to use the same emphasized word throughout a section of text, for example, it could cause the reader to lose interest, or, at worst, become irritated.

Corey Holmes's music CD cover conveys rhythm through the fragmentation of the letterforms.

In this advertisement by Heye & Partner for a German newspaper supplement, a rhythm is established in which each line of text sees two more letterforms in the title of the magazine being removed to leave the word "design."

Süddeutsche Zeitung Magazin
Nummer 16   17. April 2009
Sü deutsche Zeit ng Magazin
Sü de ts he Zeit ng Magazin
Sü de ts he eit ng Maga in
Sü de ts e eit ng M ga in
S de ts e eit ng M g in
S de s e ei n M g in
S de s e i n g in
de s i n g in
de s i g n

weniger ist mehr
Es wird Zeit, dass Gestalter und Architekten sich wieder auf das Wesentliche besinnen und den Menschen ins Zentrum ihrer Arbeit stellen. Zum 90. Jahrestag der Bauhaus-Gründung: ein Heft über die ethische Verantwortung des Designs

Visual continuity

Visual continuity is a way of leading the reader/viewer through the design and the message it conveys, making clear where parts of the design relate to each other, and thus enhancing the communication. This may be achieved by using the same typefaces for certain functions, such as chapter openings, color-coding, and consistent use of hierarchy.

There are various devices that can help visual continuity, support hierarchy, or draw attention to an aspect of the design. Examples are frames and tables, which may differentiate an area of type from the main body or create a visual link between two or more sections of text. Borders can be distracting, creating unnecessary visual noise, particularly if they are heavy or elaborate. Frames, however, may not necessarily have a border; they may simply consist of a background tint to give a more subtle effect. The same applies to tables, where too heavy a frame can almost obliterate the information the table is intended to convey. To overcome this problem, use very lightweight frames or tints. This is particularly pertinent when designing a form, whether for print or screen. Avoiding heavy borders can make the form seem less intimidating, which should encourage people to fill it in.

 Pitfall: When designing forms, remember to ensure that the frame will accommodate the maximum number of characters likely to be used.

Tools such as frames can provide opportunities for experimentation, such as the framing of decorated initial or drop caps.

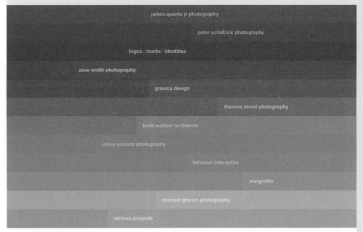

top: Miklos Kiss has used part of the Y shape as a frame for the text in this double-page spread for a fashion magazine. It provides a clean, modern, and fresh feel.

above: Organic Grid's site uses subtle graduations of color to separate the different sections of information and content.

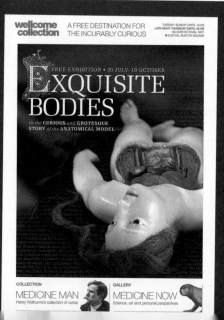

above: Absolut Vodka's logo may be identified as an image rather than words because it is so familiar.

left: The initial cap of this title is framed by a decorative surround, which provides a contrast to the rather gruesome main image. This juxtaposition helps to convey the spirit of the exhibition, which explores "the curiosities and grotesque story of the anatomical model."

Type as image

People have always played with language and letterforms for various reasons—to communicate in secret, to save time, or just for the fun of it. New technologies have led to a whole new language of acronyms and phonetic abbreviations. In texting, words are often replaced by numbers and letters that make the same sounds—for example, C U L8R for "see you later." Going one step further is the device known as a rebus, which uses a combination of images, symbols, and characters to replicate the sounds of a word or phrase. Both "textspeak" and rebuses may be used to attract attention or to give an informal feel to a design. They can also provide an opportunity for pause, as they are not always instantly decipherable.

Emoticons are another form of shorthand that uses type as image by combining punctuation and letterforms to convey meaning.

Onomatopoeia, where the sound of a word matches its meaning (for example, "buzz" or "screech"), can be extended into the visual realm, so that the typographic presentation of a word suggests its meaning. Another example of type as image, visual onomatopoeia is used extensively in cartoons and in packaging.

When text is interpreted as an image it becomes understood quickly and easily. Letterforms or sections of text may be used as objects/images in their own right or may form part of an image. These devices are often used to reinforce a message—for example, in the LG logo the "L," the "G," and a period form a friendly face. Many logotypes, such as the Absolut Vodka logo (opposite), have become identified as an image rather than words and, once established, are easily identified. Symbols and other graphic devices may also be used to replace or supplement text.

Pentagram have used a combination of letterforms and images to form this rebus of their name.

Activity

Using a short poem, nursery rhyme, or other text, replace as many words or parts of words as you can with phonetically equivalent letterforms and symbols. Make sure that you distinguish in some way between the phonetic substitutes and any words remaining from the original text.

> Hey **diddle diddle**
> The cat and **the** fiddle
> The cow jumped **over** the moon
> The little dog laughed to see such fun
> And **the** fish ran away with **the** spoon

> diddle diddle
> The 🐱 & the 🎻
> The 🐄 🐸 over the 🌙
> The little 🐴 laughed 🎲 ≈ such fun
> & the 🐟 ran away with the ⚱

In this nursery rhyme, the text to be replaced with images or symbols has been highlighted in red. For the final design, Lester Meachem provided illustrations to replace the words hey, fiddle, and jumped. He drew a shock of hay, which sounds like "hey," and a jumping frog as an ideogram for "jumped." Other images were taken from typefaces that include ornaments: Greymantle has been used for the cat and fish; the cow is from Giddyup Thangs; the moon is from Linotype Astrology; the dog and spoon from Linotype Holiday. Also from Linotype Holiday is the symbol for "sea," which sounds like "see." The picture of a die with two dots, taken from Linotype Game, replaces the word "to," which sounds like "two," and an ampersand has been used instead of the word "and."

Each of the letterforms in the title of this poster by Inkamon is derived from a classic video game—a great way to promote this festival for fans of anime, manga, and gaming.

"Never be sad for the things that have passed, smile for what is coming next."

Hourieh Nouri has drawn from the idea of emoticons to produce this poster of a smiley face made from type.

This logo for the Twins Foundation, designed by Malcolm Grear Designers, abstracts the letterforms to make an image that both represents the initials TF and conveys the idea of twins.

above: Bunch have used a rebus for the phrase "people that you like" to draw attention to this double-page spread.

right: Garrett Niksch's use of visual onomatopoeia gets the message across —"BOOM."

BOOM
Thoughts on Narrative, Destruction, and the Incursion by Truth into the Made-Up Realm
Dave King

Symbols and graphic devices

Designers frequently make use of navigational symbols and graphic devices to help understanding of information and meaning. These may include pointing fingers or arrows, ornaments, symbol typefaces such as Zapf Dingbats or Wingdings, rules, borders, and items specific to the content of the design, such as individual letterforms and fragments of images. The list may also include standard punctuation, such as exclamation marks and asterisks, and even glyphs or special characters can be used in this way. Sometimes, logos or parts of logos are used in this manner, reinforcing the brand identity.

Graphic devices do not necessarily have a navigational function. Ornaments have been incorporated into graphic designs since illuminated manuscripts, when they were often used as marginalia to decorate the page or act as reminders for the person reading the text to an audience.

Pitfall: Although symbols and graphic devices may add to a design, they can also detract from the message or content if used inappropriately or excessively. As with much design, you do not want to create noise that distracts the viewer and hinders communication of the intended message.

— A Typeface for *Noble Lettering* —

❖ Opal Pro ❖

Regular, **Bold**, *Italic* & *Script*

above: These two images show a set of ornaments that HVD Fonts have developed for the typeface Opal Pro.

below: Him have used graphic symbols in this innovative window display, which arouses curiosity as to what's on sale inside the store.

PAPER SCISSOR STONE
STORE

right: Si Scott has produced customized ornaments and symbols for this store branding.

Printing processes such as woodcut and, later, copperplate engraving and letterpress formalized many of these devices. Known as fleurons or printer's flowers, they ended up being produced as specific sets. More recently, digital typefaces incorporating a wide selection of ornaments and designs have been developed. You can also design your own ornaments either from scratch or by adapting existing images or shapes using software such as Adobe Illustrator. These can give your design a more bespoke feel and offer a contrast, particularly in Web design, to digitally produced type. There are extensive libraries of ornaments and shapes available with standard software programs such as Microsoft Word, from the Internet, or in clip-art packages.

Ornaments and graphic symbols are used on Web and print pages to create impact, to help orientation and direction, and sometimes, of course, purely for decoration.

top: TomTor and MEF designed this engaging interactive installation for Teraoka Seiko as part of the Tokyo Designers Week "container exhibition." Volunteers were weighed and then their weight was translated into a projected motion graphics experience.

above: Tom Bogman incorporates various graphic symbols and ornaments as decorative elements in this design for use on the Web.

Combinebox letterform system

by André Apel and Jan Schöttler, Austria

André Apel and Jan Schöttler have created a textual tool to complement the mainly pictographic work of street artists in urban environments, to enrich and advance their means of expression and communication.

They wanted to experiment with the typeface Schwabacher, which was used extensively from the 16th century, for example in the Lutheran Bible. They compared different versions of the typeface in order to produce an interpretation that would be suitable for use in stencil letterform.

They abstracted and sliced the letterforms to make simple shapes that harmonized with each other, creating a modular system of thirty elements that could be used in a variety of combinations but still retain their distinctive identity.

Combinebox was the master thesis of André Apel at the HfG Zürich, Switzerland, Institute Design2Context.

The individual elements of the Combinebox and how they make recognizable letterforms when used together. The elements can create both static and lively letterforms, providing opportunities for rhythm and repetition.

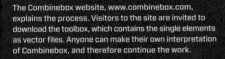

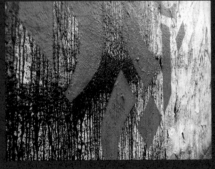

The Combinebox website, www.combinebox.com, explains the process. Visitors to the site are invited to download the toolbox, which contains the single elements as vector files. Anyone can make their own interpretation of Combinebox, and therefore continue the work.

The Combinebox system used to make stencils for street art, as below.

idegesítő, hogy minden piros lámpánál meg kell állni?

eleged van abból, hogy autóval mozdulni sem lehet csúcsforgalomban?
zavar a tény, hogy a szmog a te autódnak is köszönhető?

???
hiányzik a mozgás az életedből?
izmosabb lábakat, formásabb feneket szeretnél?
örülnél, ha tisztább lenne a levegő a városban?
gyenge az állóképességed?

szereted érezni a sebességet?
eleged van abból, hogy a szabálytalanságokért megállít a rendőr?

lassú a villamos
lassú a busz
még a metró sem elég gyors

szereted a
menetszelet
a bőrödön
érezni?

eleged van a tömegnyomorból?
hogy fel sem lehet férni a reggeli buszra

szabadabban szeretnél közlekedni?

nehezen megy a felébredés reggelenként,
unod a hónalj szagot a buszon
drága a vonaljegy

eleged van
tennél valamit
sokat kölesz?

sokat költesz az
autód szervizelésére?

nem elég a kávé, hogy magadhoz térj, valami intenzvebb kéne?
szerinted sem áll jól a fekete szín az épületeknek?

nehéz parkolóhelyet találni?

Jancsó Áron, 2008
BME, Vizuális Kommunikáció

In this poster design Áron Jancsó uses black
on yellow to create impact, and he indicates
wind rushing past a speeding cyclist by skillful
placement of type.

Chapter 5 : Color and movement

In this chapter we explore two key areas of type design: color and movement. Used imaginatively, color—of the type itself and its background—can add impact and meaning to your designs. We will discuss how to make the most of color—for example, to define hierarchy, to create balance or contrast, or to refer to the symbolic properties of certain shades. We will also look at some of the pitfalls to be avoided, such as incorporating illegible or unreadable color combinations.

Used in relation to type, the term movement can mean actual moving type, either through animation in screen-based work or by means of a mechanism to make physical, printed type alter in some way. We will consider both these aspects, as well as how to create the illusion of movement in a static piece of printed work.

Color of type

There are many ways that you can use color to create impact with type and layout. Whichever you choose, remember that colors interact and react with each other: some work together, some fight each other and cancel each other out. Also, the background and any images have to be considered as they can affect the color/s used for the type.

The way that colors work together may also have an effect on legibility. This is not always a problem: sometimes designers choose to make legibility difficult in order to attract attention to the content or when using type as a graphic element in a design.

You do not need to use bright colors to catch the eye; a subtle but strong effect may be created using monochrome, particularly if there is contrast between sections and the range of tones is explored. This is apparent in the Reuben Rosh design (opposite left), in which he has used different tints of black to emphasize the interesting shapes that the

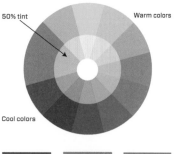

50% tint

Warm colors

Cool colors

This color wheel is intended as a reference for the various topics covered in this chapter, such as tints and complementary opposites (colors located opposite each other on the wheel). The letter tiles underneath the wheel demonstrate combinations of complementary opposites.

WWW.THEKDU.COM

trust

Stefan Lucut and Ravi Vasavan have combined strong, bright colors, which results in a striking design. The type is quite difficult to make out, but this challenge to the viewer creates visual impact.

This design by Reuben Rosh demonstrates a stylish approach to the use of grayscale or monochrome.

This website, designed by Yohannes Artinyan of i-creativ, uses a monochrome background image overlaid with simple white and gray type to create a sophisticated, understated look.

letterforms make. He has used white, dark gray, and mid-gray on a pale gray background to good effect, leaving plenty of white (or, in this case, gray) space around the type, which allows the individual items to stand out.

With the affordability and availability of full-color printing, it is tempting to make use of the full color palette on offer but, as shown in these examples, a more limited palette can make designs stand out from the crowd.

The addition of a single color to an otherwise grayscale layout can produce a dramatic effect. In the past, many designers used single color because full-color printing was expensive but, as previously discussed, this is no longer the case. Therefore, with full-color printing on display everywhere, grayscale plus a color can make a design more noticeable. Single color may take the form of a spot color, which is used to highlight or emphasize items or areas of a design, or to provide a link between elements of the design. This is often seen in magazine design where a color is selected from an image and used

for the title or other text on the page, providing cohesion and helping the reader navigate the information.

Full color may be ubiquitous but it can still create impact if used well. The combination of colors and the relationship between type, image, and background color can make all the difference. Strong color combinations such as complementary opposites or discordant pairs can create visual disturbance that brings the content out of the page or site. This is also discussed in the section on color in relation to hierarchy later in this chapter (see page 128).

TIP

If color theory is not your strong point, there are tools in some software packages, such as Adobe Illustrator, that give you menus to help you select color combinations. There are also many books and websites that provide useful information on color.

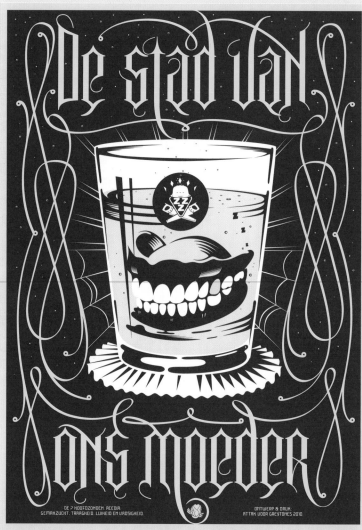

above: In this powerful poster and editorial design by Trapped in Suburbia, the strong pink would not stand out quite as much if it were not juxtaposed with the turquoise and bright green, because this combination is discordant.

right: This typically quirky design from Attak uses the same color for the type and swashes as for the gold tooth in the dentures.

below: Denzmixed have used yellow to highlight type on a complex monochrome background in this website design.

PLAYFUL

WORK. FUN. PRESS. ABOUTME.

BIOGRAPHY

Pablo Alfieri is a graphic designer and illustrator from Buenos Aires, Argentina. After working as an art director in local studios, he decided to create his own place, "Playful", where he dedicates all his passion for graphic design, illustration and typography. Characterized by a constant search of simplicity in geometries shapes, a mix between chaos and order in structures, a visual impact of colors, dinamism and finally, a strong relationship between analog and digital, lead Pablo to captivate the interest of companies like Nike, MTV International and Latinoamérica, Snickers, Chevrolet, Motorola and Nextel, agencies like W+K China, BBDO Polonia, Mother Argentina, A&P London, Cravero Lanis, Mc Cann Erikson Argentina. Recently his artworks were selected on books like "Stereographics" and "Flashback" from Victionary, "Design and Design '09" and "One Day" from Index Book, "Super Identity" from All Rights Reserved and "Typography Today" from ArtPower, magazines like "Joia Magazine", "Computer arts", "Digital Arts" and "Advanced Photoshop", and websites like "Fubiz", "NotCot", "Behance" and "CpLuv".

Pablo Alfieri es un diseñador gráfico e ilustrador nacido en Buenos Aires, Argentina. Después de trabajar como director de arte en estudios locales, decidió crear su propio lugar, "Playful" (juguetón), un espacio que le permite dedicar toda su pasión por el diseño gráfico, la ilustración y la tipografía. Caracterizado por una incesante búsqueda de la simpleza en las geometrías, una mezcla entre el caos y el orden de las estructuras, el impacto visual de los colores, el dinamismo y por último, una fuerte relación entre lo análogo y lo digital, llevo a Pablo a cautivar el interés de empresas tales como Nike, MTV Internacional y Latinoamérica, Snickers, Chevrolet, Motorola y Nextel, agencias como W+K China, BBDO Polonia, Mother Argentina, A&P Londres, Cravero Lanis y Mc Cann Erikson Argentina. Recientemente sus trabajos fueron seleccionados en libros tales como "Stereographics" y "Flashback" de Victionary, "Design and Design '09" y "One Day" de Index Book, "Super Identity" de All Rights Reserved y "Typography Today" de ArtPower, revistas como "Joia Mag", "Computer Arts", "Digital Arts" y "Advanced Photoshop", y websites tales como "Fubiz", "NotCot", "Behance" y "CpLuv"

CLIENTS
CONTACT ME

Find Playful at: Behance· flickr·   The background's photos are a project with CECILIA MOLEDO   Web Design by 4060

above: Pablo Alfieri of Playful has used powerful color combinations in the design of his website. The background image itself is made up of strong colors that he has overlaid with bright pink and green text to produce a lively, inviting design.

below: This animated sequence by Andrey Nepomnyaschev uses two primary colors with monochrome black and white, which gives the design a clean, consistent appearance.

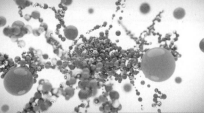

design, animation ANDREY NEPOMPYASCHEV
audio HECQ - STEELTONGUED (ULTRE STEAL TONGUES)
www.anep.ru

HIGH-SPEED TRAIN EUROPE NETWORK

above: Côme de Bouchony used tints to indicate distance and speed on this poster.

right: YuHan Keng used tints as a decorative element in this design for online publication -11magazine.

below: Ambush have used a semitransparent box over a strong background image to make the block of type legible.

far right: Oguzhan Ocalan has experimented with overlaying tints on a bright yellow background to create this powerful poster.

badona
An exclusive typeface from gravitant design studio.

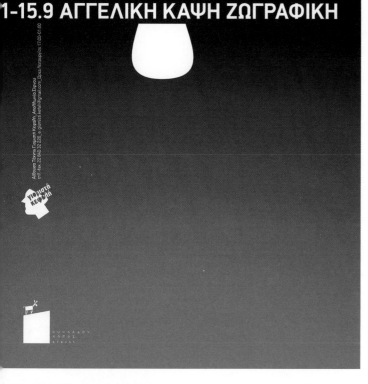

ΙΡΟΓΡΑΜΜΑ ΚΑΛΟΚΑΙΡΙ 2007
1–14.6 BRAZIL ΖΩΓΡΑΦΙΚΗ
–30.6 ΓΙΩΡΓΟΣ ΤΣΑΡΜΠΟΠΟΥΛΟΣ ΦΩΤΟΓΡΑΦΙΑ
1–14.7 AMELIE ΠΑΝΑΓΑΚΟΥ ΖΩΓΡΑΦΙΚΗ
5–31.7 ΓΙΩΡΓΟΣ ΧΑΔΟΥΛΗΣ ΖΩΓΡΑΦΙΚΗ
1–14.8 POORDESIGNERS GRAPHIC DESIGN
–14.8 ΣΟΦΙΑ ΓΕΩΡΓΟΒΑΣΙΛΗ ILLUSTRATION
5–31.8 ΑΛΕΚΟΣ ΦΑΣΙΑΝΟΣ ΖΩΓΡΑΦΙΚΗ
1–15.9 ΑΓΓΕΛΙΚΗ ΚΑΨΗ ΖΩΓΡΑΦΙΚΗ

above: Dimitris Kanellopoulos has used a gradient from black to bright pink, which reinforces the image of the lightbulb and creates a dark background for the reversed-out text.

below: Erretres chose a strong-colored background stock here, which changes the appearance of the black text and images.

Tints

A tint is a color with white added to make it lighter. Although the term derives from printing, the principle is the same in screen-based work, except that the lightening in tone is created by increasing the proportion of white light rather than white ink.

As we have mentioned before, tints are useful for differentiating areas of a design. For example, a tint may provide the background or the border for a box containing an extra or distinct piece of information.

Tints may be used for the type itself or as a background to the type, as in tables. Tints are usually represented as a percentage of the original color (where 100% is the full value of the original color and 0% is white) and most software programs will allow you to adjust these values easily.

Tints may be used to produce gradual changes from one color to another or from a color to white or black, either for the type itself or for the background. They are also used to separate a section of type from a background image—this is seen both in print and on screen where a color is made semitransparent in order to make the type legible over a strong or complicated image.

Pitfall: Be careful that your tints don't merge with the full color used; for example, yellow type on a medium tint of yellow would be difficult to identify and read.

TIP

When designing for print, take into account the color, absorbency, and texture of the paper stock, as this can change the appearance of a tint. This is an area, however, in which it is interesting to experiment.

As well as aiding navigation and legibility, tints can be used creatively as decorative elements. A word could be produced in different tints to create a pattern, or the counters of letterforms could be filled with a tint of the color used for the letters themselves.

Using color to create hierarchy

Layering of information is usually referred to as hierarchy (see page 84). Color is a useful tool for creating hierarchy both in print and on screen. One simple method, using tints, is to set the least important information in a light tint, working up in tone to the most important information in a dark tint. You could also use a strong, bright color, such as shocking pink, to attract attention to a title or a key word or phrase within the body text. The reverse may also work, where a muted color stands out from a strong, boldly colored section of text or design. Contrasting colors can be effective. They can make something stand out or, if they are complementary opposites, they may react with each other, causing the interface between the two colors to seem to vibrate. This can be effective in creating hierarchy by drawing the eye to a specific area of the design. This technique is often used in packaging—of cleaning products, for example. The same jarring effect can be achieved using discordant colors.

! **Pitfall:** Take care when using complementary opposites, such as red and green, as they can cause problems for some types of color blindness and vision problems.

above right: Nils Carlson has used the metaphor of cleaning products for this design; the link is made immediately clear to the viewer through the recreation of the bright contrasting colors associated with the packaging for this category of product.

right: The use of a strong shade of pink for the type on a light pink background makes for a striking brochure design by Karol Gadzala.

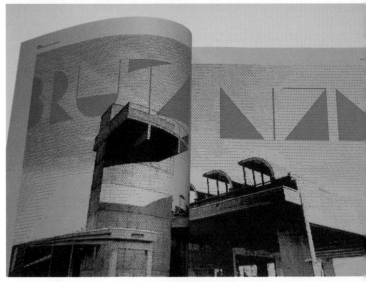

In color, as in other aspects of type design, the opposite of contrast and discord is harmony. Harmonious colors can also help create emphasis or priority of information but in a more subtle, restrained manner appropriate to subject matter, such as medical packaging or information. However, going against the grain and using harmonious colors for a product that is usually associated with contrasting, bold color combinations can make your design stand out from its rivals.

Select a pair of antonyms, such as "war" and "peace" or "quick" and "slow." Render these as a tabloid-size poster, employing color to indicate the difference between the words. For example, "war" might be red and "peace" might be pale gray on a black background.

This detail of a poster by Letman demonstrates effective use of two complementary opposite colors.

In this poster Jean-Benoît Lévy uses red type to help distinguish the word "war" from the other text, to provide a contrast and emphasize meaning.

Color and symbolism

It is almost impossible to avoid associating colors with meanings, and it is important to consider these connotations in relation to the context or subject matter of the design. One obvious link is between color and temperature: as shown on the color wheel on page 122, we think of reds and oranges as "warm" colors and blues and purples as "cold" colors. Of course, there are many other links—red as a symbol of danger or warning, black as the color of mourning. However, if you are designing for an international audience, bear in mind that color symbolism may differ between cultures. For example, in China red is associated with good fortune not danger, and the color of mourning is white not black. Regional differences aside, these allusions can help direct the reader/viewer and also convey the context or feel for the design. If your design relates to a hot climate, the obvious color choice would be within the warm range, but if you wanted to create contrast or impact, you might choose colors from the cooler range. Interestingly, placing warm colors near cool colors can make the warm color appear warmer and vice versa.

Certain colors have specific associations, which you may choose to draw on to convey your message. In designing promotional material for an ecologically concerned organization, the use of colors associated with nature or the earth, such as greens and browns, may help to support the communication. However, as mentioned before, sometimes the unexpected will help to reinforce the message, so you should experiment with the full range of colors before settling on an obvious choice.

Martin Woodtli has used warm and cool colors and a painterly style to create contrast for this poster design.

Mens Site | Girls Site | Register

PRODUCTS   BLOG   VIDEOS   TEAM   EVENTS   PLANET   COMPANY   E-SHOP

Search

Rip Curl Europe > Men's Home > Planet > Coral Guard

RIP CURL MAIL
Get the latest news, events &
promotions from Rip Curl

SIGN UP

RIP CURL STORE LOCATOR
Find your local Rip Curl

FIND

CUSTOMER SERVICE

▣ Contact Service Centre   ▣ Warranty Information

▣ Size Guides   ▣ Your Privacy

▣ Jobs

REGION SELECTOR

Europe

Your Privacy   Terms & Conditions   Contact Rip Curl   Site Map   Search Site   MyRipCurlShop.com
Use of the RIP CURL trademarks by Rip Curl. Ltd. under license from Rip Curl International Pty. Ltd.

Philippe Sain uses an "ecological" color
palette for this website for a coral-reef
conservation project sponsored by Rip Curl
Europe's Planet department.

Technical issues
relating to color

A metallic finish gives impact to this design by Zion Graphics.

Production issues will be covered in depth in chapter 7, but it is worth mentioning here some of the considerations that relate specifically to color. Color in print, for example, is reproduced differently from that on screen. In print it is usually produced using the four process color inks, cyan, magenta, yellow, and black (CMYK), whereas color for screen is produced from red, green, and blue (RGB) light. When designing on screen for print, be aware that certain colors visible on screen may not be replicable in CMYK. This is why checking color reproduction on a printed proof and making any necessary adjustments before signing off for printing is so important. Also remember that different screens display color differently—an important consideration whether you are designing for print or for screen.

Pitfall: Bear in mind the possible cumulative effect of certain combinations. For example, printing a fine serif typeface in a pale color on an absorbent stock could result in loss of detail and the type becoming unreadable.

You can select specific colors to be printed either as spot colors or as an extra color in addition to those reproduced as part of the CMYK printing process. Spot colors are specified by color reference systems, such as PANTONE®. Find the exact color you want in a swatch book, then quote its reference code to the printer or reproduction house. Spot colors are often used for company logos and identity systems. There are also various special finishes and inks, such as varnishes and metallics, which can affect the way a color appears but which also may be treated as a color. An example of this is the metallic gold lettering often used for paperback book titles.

When considering how color will print on your finished design, bear in mind that the stock can affect the depth of color. If the stock is very absorbent, for example, the color may appear less bright. The PANTONE® system shows how colors appear on different stocks, and so will help you avoid disappointing results.

Andreas Hidber has used the four process colors in their pure form to illustrate the title "Farbe Bekennen!", meaning "Show your colors!" or figuratively "Come clean!".

Type and movement

Although the term "movement" used in relation to type suggests actual moving type of the kind often found in multimedia, Web-, or screen-based design, the illusion of movement is often created in print typography using all manner of techniques, including basic flip books, blurring effects, and by the typeface design itself.

In Atelier Martino&Jaña's expressive poster the type suggests the movement and rhythm to be experienced at a jazz festival.

This poster by Small Stakes suggests movement by integrating the silhouettes of the birds with the black type.

Animated type on paper

Although most animations are now produced digitally, this used to be a largely paper-based technology, involving the painstaking sequencing of hundreds or thousands of minutely different drawings. Flip books are a relatively simple way of producing a paper animation by placing a series of pictures on each page of a book that change gradually from the first to last page. As the pages are flicked through, the images appear to move.

Animated type on screen

Flip books are one of the simplest methods of simulating movement; more complex methods are used in traditional cell animation and movie titles. More recently, sophisticated software has enabled designers to experiment with moving type for a range of screen-based contexts, from smartphone apps to TV ads. Although the production of moving type often entails the acquisition of specialist technical or software skills, the type designer's basic principles of legibility and readability should not be forgotten.

The most straightforward approach to moving type is scrolling, which involves type gradually moving up, down, or across the screen, as commonly seen in movie and TV titles and website banners. This method is still used extensively in movie credits, but many people don't tend to see these as they either turn off the TV or leave the theater as soon as the action has finished. Perhaps to maintain audience interest, more complex animations have now been developed where the letterforms are manipulated— to appear from the background, for example, or to fade in and out, or move around the screen. Such animations often incorporate images or may even form part of an animated image. Early examples were hand produced, whereas nowadays they tend to be created digitally. In character animation, such as Nick Park's *Creature Comforts* which are hand modeled and use stop-frame animation rather than computer-generated imagery (CGI), traditional techniques give a different feel to the animation. Compare Saul Bass's animated title sequence for *The Man with the Golden Arm* with the CGI titles for, say, *Fantastic Four:* the former has a more tactile, immediate quality, whereas the latter has a slicker, more artificial feel.

In some cases the type is stationary but the camera moves to give the effect of the type being part of a landscape or a structure. In other cases animated type is projected onto

Activity

Choose a word (a relatively long one works best). Put one letter of the word on a sheet of paper, then design a series of pages that reveal the word by one letter per page, ending up with the full word on the last page. Make sure that the letters are in the same position on each page. Fasten the pages together along the spine and then flick through them to see the word gradually materialize. It is best to use a semitransparent paper such as layout paper or photocopying paper, so that you can trace the letters onto each page.

A simple flip book in action.

above: Melvin Galapon has used a digitized version of the flip-book technique for this series of animated postcards.

below: Blac Ionica have used stop-frame animation to produce this short film advertising a television food channel.

static objects or surfaces, such as buildings, to change appearance or attract attention. This technique is often seen in art and design installations.

Moving type is often included in website design, either as part of the main screen or as a separate "pop-up," to enable more information to be delivered in a small space. Apps are another vehicle for this sort of animation, to be found, for example, in the pop-up advertisements that often accompany free downloads. This is similar to the small ads that scroll across the edge of the pages in some online newspapers and magazines.

Animated versions of logos are generated for multimedia applications and TV ads to create impact. An example is the animated cartoon letterforms used for products aimed at children.

Sophisticated software, and powerful delivery platforms such as smartphones, have enabled designers and artists to realize their most experimental and creative ideas. Type can become part of a virtual reality, letterforms can seamlessly morph into the most unlikely objects— imagination is the only limitation.

STRUT

25 YEARS OF THE BEST OF BRITISH FASHION · 1ST OCTOBER · 25TH DECEMBER 2009

V&A

left: Although this poster by Jonathan Arundel is not animated, its high-gloss finish means that reflections of people moving past it will cause the surface to be constantly changing.

below: Ellen Zhao has introduced an animated element to this printed booklet to give it an interactive, lively feel.

above: In this use of type in the environment, Small have optimized the corrugated surface to give an impression of movement as the viewer passes by.

right: These images show examples from Tobias Battenberg's project projecting letterforms in Akzidenz Grotesk typeface onto structures in the urban landscape.

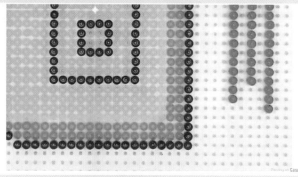
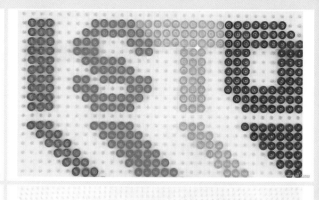

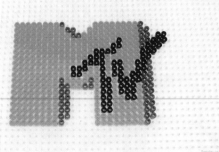

above: Todd Smith animated the MTV logo using a plastic craft system that would be familiar to many children.

left: This early example of virtual animation from the late 1980s–early 1990s, Legible Cities by Jeffrey Shaw, uses type as virtual three-dimensional architecture, which the viewer explores by pedaling on a static bicycle in the real world.

d.kele has produced this innovative design
in which freeborders hold up various
shapes, including letterforms, made
out of illuminated tubes.

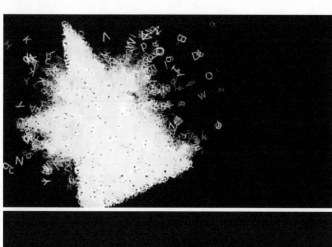

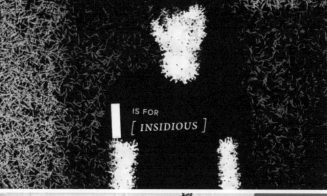

left: Brent Barson's multimedia project "F is for Fail" uses the alphabet to produce a typographic representation of a person's creative process.

opposite: Julien Breton uses moving light to produce these Arabic letterforms.

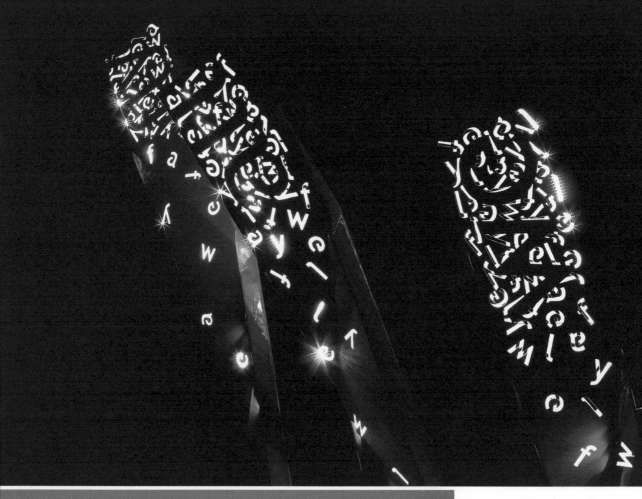

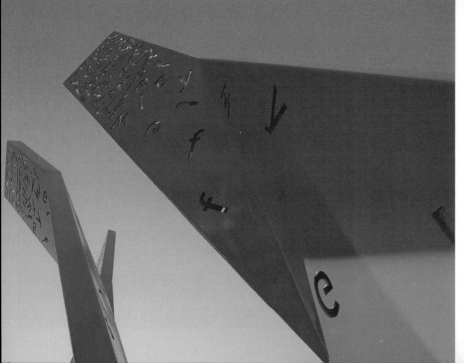

this page: The letterforms covering this sculpture by Sanjeev Shankar come to life when illuminated at night.

opposite: Yorgo Tloupas has adapted the rotating mechanism of airport departure boards for use with skis to attract attention to this window display.

Issues associated with moving type

There are particular considerations in relation to legibility and readability associated with moving type. Flickering screens or lights may be particularly challenging for people with vision problems. Color blindness affects many people and may be relevant to your design, especially if it is conveying important information such as a warning. As with any design, it is important to understand the needs of your audience, and appreciate social and ethical issues, at the same time as developing a creative and/or experimental design. It is up to you to decide which techniques are appropriate to the content and avoid using something just because you can. If moving type is overused it can be distracting and, in the case of website design, can cause delay in pages opening, leading to frustration and the risk of the audience moving elsewhere. Having said this, moving type has exciting potential for attracting an audience and conveying information quickly and effectively.

Transitions

Building a transition—from one piece of text to another, or from an image to a piece of text or vice versa—is a useful way to draw attention to a design. The technique can add humor, impart a meaning, establish emphasis or hierarchy, rhythm or repetition. It can also work with a narrative, such as in cartoons, or act as a counterpoint to a narrative. Low-tech contexts for transitional type include flick billboards and airport information signage. More advanced examples include LED grids that light up according to the information required—often used for announcements in railroad stations.

There are many examples of built-in facilities and tools for making transitions, such as those available in Microsoft's Powerpoint presentation package.

 Pitfall: When using effects and styles built into software, stand back and consider your motives. Does the effect contribute to your message, or does it just show that you know how to do it? Does it add to or detract from the overall impact of your design?

Moving

This change-of-address mailout card by
The Chase uses an ingenious transition and
folding arrangement to communicate the
message that the *Manchester Evening News*
headquarters is moving and expanding.

Manchester Evening News

The Manchester Evening News,
Manchester Metro News, Metro,
Channel M, Manchester Online,
Jobs North West, CV Station,
one large family expanding into
one big brilliant new building.

From 2nd October 2006
Number 1 Scott Place, Manchester
M3 3RN ① 0161 832 7200

above: In this experimental piece, Andrew van der Merwe allows time and the elements to change his original type design.

below: Livius Dietzel applies type to fruit and records the effects as the fruit decays in this time-lapse-inspired project.

Static but changing

You can achieve innovative, meaningful effects by placing static type in a setting where it will be affected by physical processes such as erosion, precipitation, or decay. By filming or photographing the type over time, you can record the changes that it undergoes for use in print or multimedia applications. This technique is particularly useful for conveying abstract themes such as space, time, or impermanence.

Implying movement

At the beginning of this chapter there is a good example by Áron Jancscó of type being used to imply movement (see page 120). The type is used to represent a moving object as well as the effect of movement. This can be a way of conveying meaning, giving life to a design, directing the viewer, or even making a transition. Creating an illusion like this provides an ideal opportunity for experimentation —for example, with combinations of typefaces, point sizes, and type families.

Viewpoint

Movement can be created or implied in static type by the way the type is positioned in relation to the audience's viewpoint. This technique may be used in signage and billboards where the spectator is transient or the signage is in an unusual position in relation to the spectator. The type may be on a moving object such as the side of a truck. Sometimes a series of posters or similar are designed to be viewed sequentially by a moving audience, almost like a simple animation. An example of this would be a series of posters running along an escalator shaft, where the message is conveyed through viewing the entire sequence. Another way of implying movement is by altering a poster over a series of weeks or an ad in a magazine over successive pages or issues. There are many opportunities for using viewpoint creatively; experiment with as many possibilities as you can think of. These techniques may be used to create different effects such as surprise, shock, or a sense of complicity—the audience may feel privileged to be in on the game and enjoy monitoring the gradual revelation of meaning.

left: Frost Design have used a light typeface and arranged the letterforms to reinforce the movement associated with dance.

Activity

Choose three words associated with movement in some way (we've used "elastic," "zip," and "wriggle") and experiment with producing them in a range of typefaces, families, and sizes to help reinforce the movement implied by the word.

These experiments show the use of different typefaces, family members, and sizes to help reinforce the words' meanings. Memphis has been used for "zip" because its slab serifs suggest the interlocking parts of a zipper; Univers has been chosen for "elastic" because its extensive family allows experimentation with width to indicate stretch; Brioso has been selected for "wriggle" because of the fluidity of its italic form, which is evocative of wriggling.

In this installation Moshik Nadav has devised a spiral timeline associated with the kidnapping of Israeli soldier Gilad Shalit in 2006. Each poster records a separate event in terms of the number of days, hours, minutes, and seconds into Shalit's captivity that the event took place. The posters are arranged in chronological order as the viewer ascends the staircase.

The words in this design by Pentagram seem to surge out from the doorway as viewers approach. This sense of thrust and energy works well for an inspirational motto in a New York school.

This rotating sign by Pentagram is viewed differently depending on whether it is seen from immediately below or from a distance.

Jesus Iso
by Thomas Pavitte, Melbourne

This typography project by Thomas Pavitte involved experimenting with 3-D using Google Sketchup. In the first stage Thomas created vector shapes in Adobe Illustrator using the letters of his name. He exported them into Sketchup and extruded the shapes.

After these initial experiments Thomas began work on a bigger project, *Jesus Iso*, which was based on the lyrics of the song "Jesus Etc." by Wilco. The lyrics refer to tall buildings, and Thomas responded by developing his letterforms to resemble buildings in a futuristic cityscape.

Thomas took an organic approach to the design, allowing the typeface to evolve in response to the shapes and images conjured up by the lyrics. He didn't want any spaces between letters or words, so individual letterforms needed several alternative shapes to allow them to fit together.

Each letterform was extruded individually in Google Sketchup, which enabled Thomas to vary the height of each shape. To maximize the contrast between the letterforms, he tried to place taller shapes next to smaller ones.

This design was exported back to Illustrator and converted to vector format for completion. Thomas created several layers so that he could change sections of the same color easily.

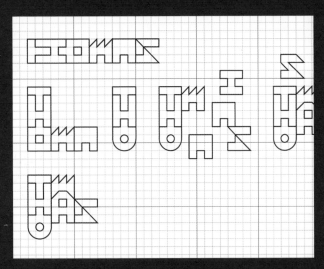

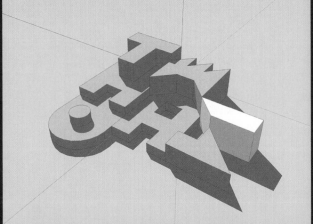

above: Preliminary sketches and experiments with letterforms.

above right: Initial extruded shapes in Google Sketchup.

right: The extrusions were exported back into Illustrator and refined.

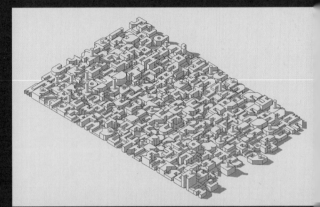

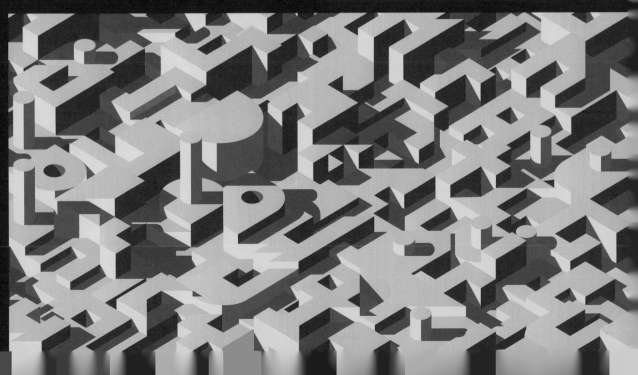

clockwise from above: Variations on individual letterforms.

Thomas used a grid to help draw the letterforms for the phrase "Jesus don't cry."

Completed text in 2-D, which was intended to give the impression of organized chaos.

An isometric view of the words in Google Sketchup before adding color.

The finished piece creates an abstract pattern based on 3-D letterforms.

150

Las letras no forman solo palabras.
Forman ideas, ideologías, sentimientos,
y también,
REVOLUCIONES

Colorless created this portrait of Che
Guevara using nothing but type.

Chapter 6 : Experiments with type

In this chapter we will investigate the creative and expressive potential of type. This will include experimental techniques for print and screen, such as calligraphy, embossing, and printmaking. It will also cover the use of a range of media and experiments with, for example, surface treatment, texture, and modeling. We will explore these experimental approaches and techniques in the context of applications such as store signage, webpages, packaging, and public art.

Experimental techniques

Experimenting with type has been discussed throughout this book: this section looks at some different approaches to experimenting with type. Expressive letterforms may be used to convey meaning or add emphasis. For example, you might use a large heavy typeface, such as Impact, to reinforce a sense of gravity. Having settled on the typeface itself, you might also try out family variations, such as bold to indicate strength or italic to indicate movement. These are obvious choices, but it is worth experimenting with a large range of typefaces and families, and also thinking unconventionally to make the audience look twice; a simple example would be using a delicate script face for a word that conveys weight, such as "elephant."

As well as experimenting with existing typefaces and families to reinforce a message, you can also play with meaning in different ways. Typograms, which use type as a visual way of encapsulating an idea, have been around in the form of logos and trademarks for many years. They provide an opportunity to experiment with interpretation of words. A typogram can be used to convey a lot of information in a small space. As a simple example, a logo for a fish market could be the name of the market produced in the shape of a fish (see above left).

Another way of communicating quickly is to replace one letter of a word or phrase with an image that helps to reinforce the message: this is often referred to as "the missing letter." As with typograms, these provide lots of opportunities to experiment, take risks, and investigate the potential offered by different media. For example, the "o" in the word "roll" (as in bread roll) could be replaced by a bread roll and then be photographed and digitally modeled, or it could be produced with a facsimile bread roll as a three-dimensional sign.

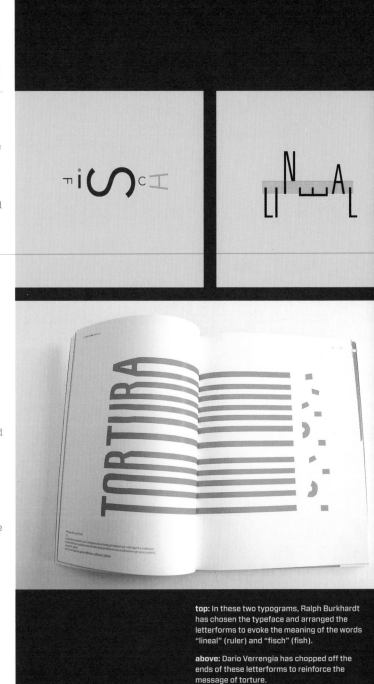

top: In these two typograms, Ralph Burkhardt has chosen the typeface and arranged the letterforms to evoke the meaning of the words "lineal" (ruler) and "fisch" (fish).

above: Dario Verrengia has chopped off the ends of these letterforms to reinforce the message of torture.

top: The use of an image of a zipper to replace the letter "i" in the word "unzipped" reinforces the message and has resulted in a strong display piece by The Consult.

left: Even with two missing letters (replaced by quotation marks), Lee Stokes's clever treatment of the word "speech" is still legible and conveys the message.

speech™

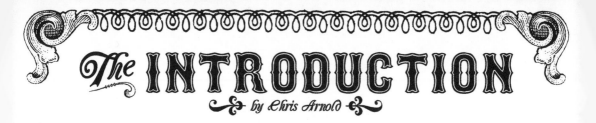

The INTRODUCTION
by Chris Arnold

CREATIVE ORCHESTRA

IS THE FIRST ANGLO SPANISH ADVERTISING AGENCY.
WE PRACTICE A POLICY OF

DIVERSITY

And

HAVE FOUND THAT BY WORKING WITH CREATIVES FROM MANY NATIONS
AND CULTURES WE ARE ABLE TO THINK IN A DIFFERENT WAY. EACH CREATIVE
BRINGING A DIFFERENT APPROACH, EACH LEARNING FROM ONE ANOTHER.
TO DATE WE HAVE HAD PEOPLE FROM

20 NATIONS

UNLIKE THE AVERAGE LONDON AGENCY WE PRACTICE A POLICY TO TRY
AND HAVE EQUAL NUMBERS OF

MEN & WOMEN

ONE REASON, OF MANY, WHY WE RECENTLY WON CREATIVE BRIEFS
PROMOTING KING OF SHAVES NEW MALE AND FEMALE RANGES.

Experiment with missing-letter designs: choose a word and devise an effective, meaningful way of replacing one letter with an image. This may be done digitally or manually or by a combination of the two.

above: In this piece Petar Pavlov has replaced the letter "o" with a drilled hole to exemplify the meaning of the word "hole."

Pastiche, the quoting of a particular style or look, can be an effective way to make a historical, cultural, or contextual reference. The technique relies on your ability to identify and recreate visual reference points, of which typefaces are a particularly evocative example. For example, if you wanted to evoke the Art Deco era, you might use a typical typeface of the period such as Bifur. Depending on the context and the relationship between typography and content, a pastiche may be interpreted as a homage to a particular style, person, or period, or it may be satirical in intention, or even have deliberate negative connotations. Applying a "retro" style to a modern-day communication can be an effective way of associating your message with the spirit of the period you are quoting. Again, this is worth experimenting with, as sometimes an obscure reference will make an audience pay more attention than an obvious one.

! **Pitfall:** If using pastiche, take care not simply to copy or replicate the past. Pastiche is a way of referencing the past by using relevant styles, techniques, or even cultural icons.

above left: Ragnar Freyr has drawn on the clean, stylish geometric lines of 1920s/'30s type design for this poster advertising a dance-music event.

below: Joan Ot Comellas has taken an illustrative approach to the logo on the banner of this outdoor pursuits webpage, replacing the letter "i" with a graphic of a climber on a rope.

These examples of architectural signage
show the contrast in style and approaches
between a Victorian façade and a modern sign
by Fons Hickmann m23.

Type out there

As you make your way through any 21st-century town or
city, you will find type, or things that look like letterforms,
all around you. The most obvious category is signage, of
which there is so much, particularly in built-up areas, that
often we don't register it or its message. Just think of how
many times you try to pull open a door despite the sign
that clearly says "push," or vice versa. Next time you're in
a town center, make a conscious effort to focus on all the
type around you that you normally ignore (taking care not
to get run over!), as this exercise will help develop your
visual awareness and your instinct for experimentation.

Signage has to compete with so much other information
and therefore, as with advertising, its message may be
diluted or even negated. However, signs can be a rich
source of inspiration. Even examples you consider to be
poor can suggest alternative approaches or, at the very
least, how *not* to do it. Signage is, or should be, site-specific
and functional. For example, a freeway road sign has to
convey sometimes quite complex information within a
matter of seconds as cars speed past it. It is interesting to
study the sorts of typefaces that make effective signs, the
most obvious being the ubiquitous Helvetica, and to
experiment with size, shape, and color in relation to the
location of the sign. For example, a green, leaf-shaped sign
might not be the most eye-catching choice for a wooded
setting. Consider all kinds of examples: store signage,
public signage, or even "beware of the dog" or "please shut
the gate" signs.

Another form of type in the environment is graffiti, which
can range from vandalism to art. At its most basic, graffiti
is a scrawl on a wall but it has developed, particularly in
urban areas, into a method of using type creatively. Graffiti
style has been replicated and refined for use in many
typefaces, such as Scrawler produced by Graffitifonts,
and has inspired many designs. Its association with youth
culture and urban style makes graffiti-like typography
ideal for communicating with, or advertising to, young,
urban audiences. Examples may be found in the music,
fashion, and club industries, particularly hip-hop music,
which is synonymous with graffiti-style type.

Many tattoos have similar cultural links but tattooing is
usually more personal than graffiti, and certainly more

above: Thirst have employed strong color and distinctive materials to provide contrast in an urban environment where concrete and glass predominate.

below: Always be on the alert for inspiration. Hand-produced, impromptu lettering, as seen on this "Beware Lambs" sign, can provide a refreshing alternative to "designed" signage.

below: Prima 09 is a typeface by Welab Designers intended to look like graffiti.

Ale Paul's typeface was inspired by traditional
tattoos and he uses this link to advertise it
and show how it works in a setting.

permanent (and painful). Although there are traditional
letterforms used in tattooing, it has a strong calligraphic
influence and the stylus allows the tattooist to follow a
creative idea or experiment with line and shade (with the
recipient's agreement). It is a rich source of inspiration and
has been used extensively in advertising and media.

Type is found in many shapes and forms on most ephemera:
the stuff of everyday life can provide surprises and ideas
for the creative use of type. Ephemera can range from a
bus ticket or postage stamp to a movie poster or piece of
packaging and can be in different languages, alphabets,
printed on different materials, or hand produced. Nowadays,
there is also digital ephemera, which you can collect as
bookmarks or screenshots. A collection of ephemera can
be a rich resource for generating concepts, evaluating
materials, or just appreciating different ways of using type.

Letterforms are not only to be found in type: viewed
imaginatively, the tines of a fork could become a letter "E";
a pointed tower could transform itself into an "A"; or the
branches of a tree could make a "Y" shape. Train your
antennae to pick up this accidental alphabet all around
you. These letterforms may appear whole or be formed by
cropping or manipulating a photograph of an object or
shape. Such forms could be used individually as part of a
design, as in the "missing letter" (see page 155), developed
into phrases or full alphabets, or just collected for inspiration.

above: Grouping ephemera by letter,
as in this collection of found three-
dimensional representations of the
letter "u," can provide a focus for your
research and a stimulus for experiment.

left: Ivan Khmelevsky uses a tattoo-
inspired design to promote an
exhibition on the theme of skin.

Activity

Collect examples of images from the environment that look like
letterforms. You can use found images from magazines, or take your
own photographs or use other people's (with permission). When you
have examples for each letter of the alphabet, assemble them into a
poster either for print or screen.

Because there are four more squares in
this grid than there are letters in the Latin/
Roman alphabet, this alphabet drawn from
nature and the built environment begins and
ends with a single quotation mark. It also
includes an extra Z and an ellipsis (...) to
complete the grid.

This series of photographs, by Jim Lind,
records the designer's search for everyday
objects that resemble the letter "O."

mehr für die
mit weniger!
Mein Paradies ist die
Hölle auf Erden! Mehr
Millionen für Millionen! Pa
rolen für Marode! Ich bin das
Ozonloch! Atomkraft
wegbeissen! Lange
weile wegmessern!

The calligraphy of Mi Fu gives a traditional but dynamic feel to this website by the National Palace Museum, Taiwan.

Felix Vorreiter has developed a handheld tool that generates automated graffiti text.

Self-generated experiments

As well as finding shapes that indicate letterforms, you can also modify existing letterforms or create your own —either by hand or digitally, or by a combination of the two. A wide range of media, tools, skills, and techniques can be applied to letterforms and type. For example, graffiti is often produced using spray paint, but there are many examples of instant graffiti produced in chalk or marker pen. The surface texture plays an important role in the appearance of the letterforms: a brick or concrete wall will have a more prominent texture than a metal panel.

Derived from the Greek for "beautiful writing," calligraphy is a traditional method of producing letterforms that is still widely used today, both formally and experimentally. There are typefaces designed to replicate or suggest calligraphy or at least handwriting. Some cultures have a strong relationship with calligraphy. For example, beautiful typography is particularly valued in the Arab world because Islam prohibits the use of images. There is also a strong calligraphic tradition in Asia, which has informed the development of other art forms in other cultures; Picasso and Matisse both acknowledged the influence of Chinese calligraphy in their work. Calligraphy can be produced using the simplest of tools, such as a quill or even a stick. Try out a range of writing implements, inks, and other media and materials to write on. The absorbency and texture of the surface, the density of the ink, and the scale of the work will all affect the result.

Another traditional method for rendering type is engraving, where letterforms are cut into a surface. The engraving may be the finished product in its own right or serve as a template to be inked up and printed from.

The opposite of engraving is relief printing, where the background is cut away to leave the letterforms raised. Traditional letterpress printing (see page 10) is an example of this technique. Letterpress printers still exist, but you can also use the type in a freer way. A quick and fun approach is to experiment with children's printing sets or rubber stamps. Alternatively, design your own letterforms for relief printing by means of the simple potato print (see page 57) or by creating linocut or woodblock prints.

Letman has used a formal style of calligraphy to add a decorative element to this interior space.

Stencils, where ink is pushed through a mask, can create interesting effects; again the surface texture and the medium used will play an important part in the end result. Stenciling can vary in complexity and scale, from dabbing paint through a simple shape cut out of paper to commercial silkscreen printing operations.

Letraset® sheets or other transfer systems provide another interesting area for experiment. Try using them to form new letter shapes or combining letterforms to exploit the way the transfers often break up or deteriorate. Although superseded by digital publishing technologies, some transfer-lettering systems are still available in a limited range of typefaces.

Photocopying is a great way to reproduce letterforms in different sizes, so that you can cut them up and reposition them. Repeated photocopying leads to distressing, which can yield unexpected results and give an immediate, hand-produced feel to a design. Scanning can be used in a similar way, with greater scope for digital manipulation.

Remember that type design doesn't have to be two-dimensional. Physical modeling and the digital equivalent allow you to add substance to a design. This may be an actual or virtual presence or it could be a photograph of a model. There are all kinds of ways of modeling physical type: try squeezing toothpaste or paint from a tube, forming trails of sand or salt, or building structures out of cardboard or foam. Screen-based modeling can be as simple as applying a shadow to give a letterform depth or as complex as creating intricate matrices for computer games or virtual worlds. Combining the physical and the virtual, or the three-dimensional and the two-dimensional, can work well. For example, you might project holographic type onto a three-dimensional form.

The advantage of using physical materials is that the nature of the media can produce unexpected results. A misalignment in stencil printing, for example, can throw up all sorts of creative opportunities. Materials themselves, and the actions on them, such as the friction of pencil on paper, can dictate the range of marks possible and can impose boundaries on what you do; but sometimes it is the need to overcome a limitation that leads to the most inventive outcomes.

above: Yani Arabena uses a traditional relief-printing process to produce a calligraphic poster.

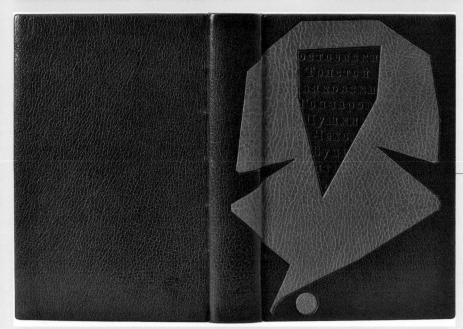

left: Paolo Taddeo has used traditional leather tooling techniques to produce this stylish contemporary book cover.

below left: Eurico Sá Fernandes uses experimental relief printing to give an individual feel to business cards.

below right: NB Studio employ letterpress design to produce strong typographic shapes.

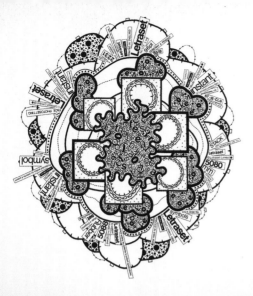

left: Kelly Mark has used old transfer lettering to produce this experimental piece.

below left: Barbara Brownie creates typographic patterns using images of three-dimensional letterforms.

below: abgc have formed text using white Lego® blocks set on a background of different colored pieces. By using a much-loved medium in an unusual context, the designers immediately create interest.

left: Stormhand modeled letterforms into three-dimensional shapes and animated them to create an exciting moving image for the 40th anniversary of Amnesty International.

Surfaces

The surface of the material on which lettering is produced
can make a massive difference to the finished product.
Sometimes the way that you apply lettering to a surface
can physically change that surface. Examples of this kind
of transformative process include embossing and debossing.

When you emboss a section of a design, the area is raised
above the surface of the stock. A deboss has the opposite
effect; the area is impressed into the stock. Both techniques
create texture in a design and can make as much of an
impression on the audience as on the stock. They are
most commonly performed industrially, but you can also
manage them yourself, with a little practice, on a variety of
materials. Paper folding and cutting, often seen in pop-up
books, can be used in a similar way to embossing to raise
the surface texture. Again, this requires some practice and
research into techniques.

Raised areas may also be achieved by incorporating
different materials, such as fabrics, and different
techniques, such as stitching and collage. Be adventurous
with materials: there are all sorts of alternatives to
traditional stock, such as plastic, glass, ceramic, textile,
wood, metal, foam—there's no limit as long as you can
work with it. If you want to use type produced on an
unconventional surface, you could photograph or scan
it and then import it into a design for print or screen.

above: Mission Design used debossing
to create this logotype on a packaging
sleeve. The debossing reinforces the illusion
of three-dimensionality.

right: Aaron Alexander's design for the British
Dog Association's Annual Report incorporates
an embossed bone motif, which provides a
tactile quality as well as using gentle humor
to attract attention.

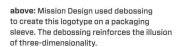

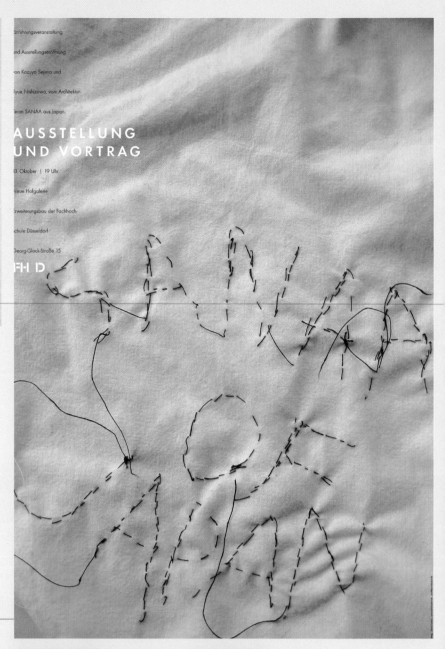

above: This pop-up alphabet by Ron King gives an effect similar to embossing in the way it reflects light and shade.

above right: Daniel Taubert uses hand-stitched lettering to provide contrast in this poster design.

right: Part of the Instant Hutong art project, this large sheet, a detail of which is shown here, carries a stylized map of a densely populated district of old Beijing. The tufting technique used here would lend itself to letterforms and could work well in a variety of contexts, including advertising banners.

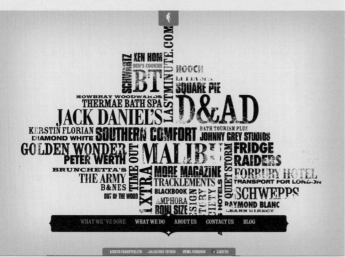

left: A distressed typeface has been used for the opening pages of Kerve's website to give it a rough, immediate quality.

TIP If you produce three-dimensional type for use in a two-dimensional design, it is usually better to take a carefully lit digital photograph and import the photograph directly, rather than to make a scan, as scanning can have a flattening effect.

As discussed in relation to photocopying, distressing can change the surface of a design. This may be achieved by many different means, including smudging, scratching, beating, applying a corrosive material, or by exposing it to the elements to produce weathering effects such as fading, rot, or rust. All these processes may be simulated using digital technology. Another interesting digital effect is solarization (see below), which appears to change the surface by reversing tones—making dark areas light and vice versa.

Light can have an impact on how texture or surface is perceived. For example, a subtle embossing technique such as blind embossing may not be obvious without a directional light to throw some shadow and therefore define the shape. Some software packages provide simulated embossing with adjustable light sources to give different effects. Light may also affect highly reflective materials such as glass and chrome. This needs to be taken into account when designing with such materials, and can often be exploited to produce interesting effects.

above left: Alejandra Román has used the qualities of distressed photocopying to create a textural and sophisticated book design.

left: When a straightforward black-and-white photograph of boot- and paw-prints in sand (far left) is manipulated using a digital solarize filter (left), the tonal values are reversed and the image made to look quite different.

Type in three dimensions

Letterforms may be produced in three-dimensional format for a variety of reasons; one of the most ubiquitous is signage, particularly for storefronts and business premises. Such letterforms may be produced individually or as bas-relief (elements are carved or sculpted in low relief or in some way raised from a flat background).

Other everyday examples of three-dimensional letterforms include fridge magnets, letter-shaped pasta, badges, and logos on items such as cars or white goods. Such examples provide opportunities for experimentation and reinterpretation, inviting your audience to see commonplace things in new ways.

There are many examples of three-dimensional type used in sculpture. You can see examples in public art or in galleries and museums. Neon lettering has been used for art by contemporary artists such as Jenny Holzer and Tracey Emin, as well as for signage on buildings—nowhere more so than in Las Vegas. In many instances, neon tubing is now being superseded by LED and plasma screens, which have the advantage of being more energy-efficient and cheaper to produce, as well as being more versatile in that they can carry moving as well as static type.

An example of a more functional usage is signage-lettering systems such as the ones used in large hotels to direct delegates to the right conference room. These provide a readable, easy-to-update alternative to a handwritten list on a whiteboard.

Three-dimensional lettering offers great potential for creative approaches and hands-on experimentation. This may be through the quoting of existing letterforms, or by creating your own letterforms from almost anything. A wide range of materials and media can be manipulated and used to create customized typefaces, words, or just individual letterforms to be used for emphasis or to draw attention to the content.

Pop-up books and other forms of paper engineering such as origami offer opportunities for experimentation in three-dimensional form and allow a transition from two to three dimensions. Such artifacts can engage an audience through their novelty and interactivity.

below: This traditional three-dimensional store signage for R.B. Shah & Co. stands out among the many other signs and distractions in this busy Ahmedabad street.

bottom: Fons Hickmann m23 exploited the contrast between bas-relief and engraving in this signage system for the Mercedes-Benz Museum in Stuttgart. The numberforms that indicate location are raised and made out of polished metal, which makes them stand out dramatically from the unused numberforms, which are incised.

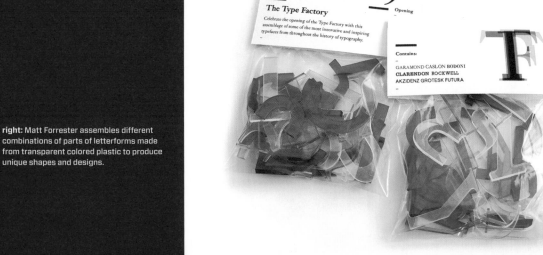

right: Matt Forrester assembles different combinations of parts of letterforms made from transparent colored plastic to produce unique shapes and designs.

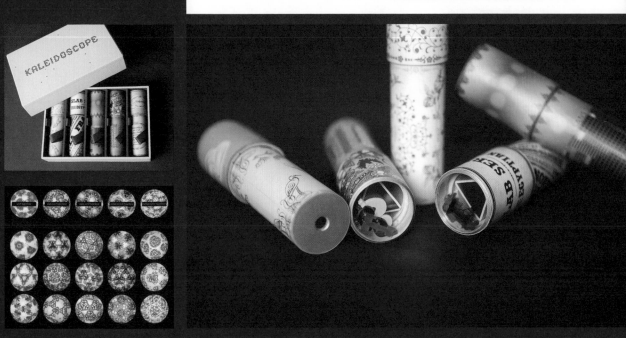

These four images show an exciting and experimental kinetic use of three-dimensional lettering by Katerina Orlikova. Taking the principle of the classic toy kaleidoscope, she used plastic molded three-dimensional letterforms in different colors and typefaces (serif, sans serif, ornamental, etc.) to form patterns as the kaleidoscope is shaken and gyrated. As you can see above, the different typeface forms produce radically different shapes and patterns.

left: This sign by Studio Oscar is formed by neon lighting. It uses the luminous qualities of neon to reinforce the word "Brill."

center left: This response by Stewart Walker and Alasdair Griffiths to a D&AD competition brief to promote a series of print-on-demand film books for Faber & Faber subverts classic cinema signage to humorous and intriguing effect.

below left: Martin Woodtli has combined images of text in the environment to create movement and immediacy in this design. The brightness of the main word, "lichtecht," evokes its meaning: "non-fade."

below: In this piece by Juan Camilo Rojas, the letterforms themselves are integral to the sculpture. They are formed from rusted nails, which stand out from the shorter, shinier nails of the background to produce an innovative bas-relief effect.

right: Amandine Alessandra has used the human body as the basis for a typeface, which she has applied in print- and Web-based design.

below left: Brian Banton takes a novel approach to pop-ups, using the pop-up strips to reveal hidden text.

below right: Plastic pop-out lettering is often used for temporary signage in hotels and conference venues.

right: This double-page spread by Benja Harney shows how pop-up technology can be applied to type.

Zim and Zou manipulated strips of paper to form three-dimensional calligraphic shapes.

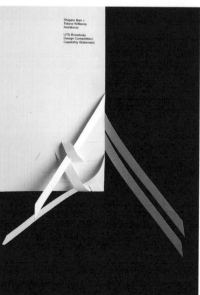

Benja Harney and Gregory Anderson used a sophisticated piece of paper engineering to produce this visually dynamic letterhead.

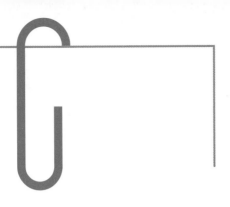

Type as image

We have discussed various ways of using type as image in chapter 4: emoticons, rebuses, textspeak, closure, and visual onomatopoeia (see pages 113–115). Calligrams and concrete poetry are another, engaging example of type as image, in which the shape of the layout of a poem is as important as the content in conveying meaning. Calligrams and concrete poetry can also be combined with other techniques such as rhythm and repetition to aid communication.

above: Thirst have used the shape of a paperclip to represent the letter G here.

below: Lost in Space show how calligrams can translate from art into advertising in their animated screen-based design for a phone-recycling campaign.

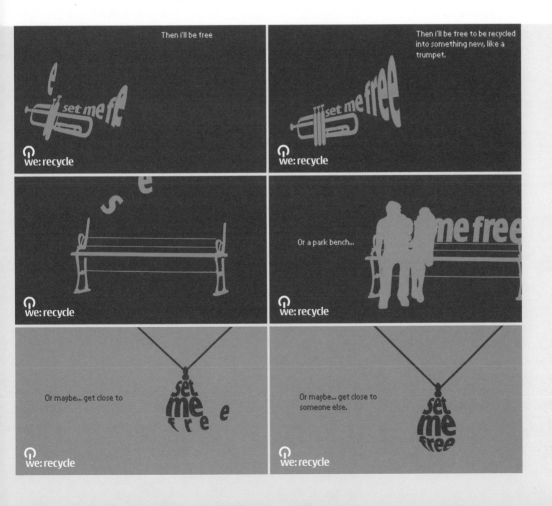

Pattern and decoration

Experimentation can result in accidental patterns derived from individual letterforms or combinations of letterforms. Patterns can establish a visual rhythm that draws the viewer into a design (see page 110). Letterforms, which are usually regular in shape, lend themselves to this sort of manipulation.

This kind of patterning technique can transform letterforms into abstract shapes. It can add layers of meaning, particularly when used to create logotypes (see page 113). Some packaging is designed so that the individual products form a pattern when they are stacked on supermarket shelves or other point-of-purchase displays.

Letterforms have been used decoratively at least since the ornate initial capitals seen in medieval manuscripts (see below). Even with such a long tradition, decorated initials can still be incorporated in novel ways to lend impact to a design. Developments in illustration software make the construction of complex illustrated forms more accessible and open up a range of creative opportunities for expressing ideas. This sort of abstraction and image-making blurs the boundaries between type and image.

above: In this design by Dario Verrengia, a complex pattern has been produced by repeating a single word.

below left: The beautiful initial capitals in this illuminated manuscript that would have taken many hours to produce can be emulated in a fraction of the time using modern digital technology.

below: Paul Grabowski has create decorative and complex poster u formed from type.

Take one letterform in a specific typeface. (Choose any letterform you like, but the "g" in Minion Pro lends itself well.) Form patterns with it using any of the techniques discussed in this book. You could repeat it, rotate it, or invert it, combine different sizes or weights, produce it in different colors or tints—anything that comes to mind.

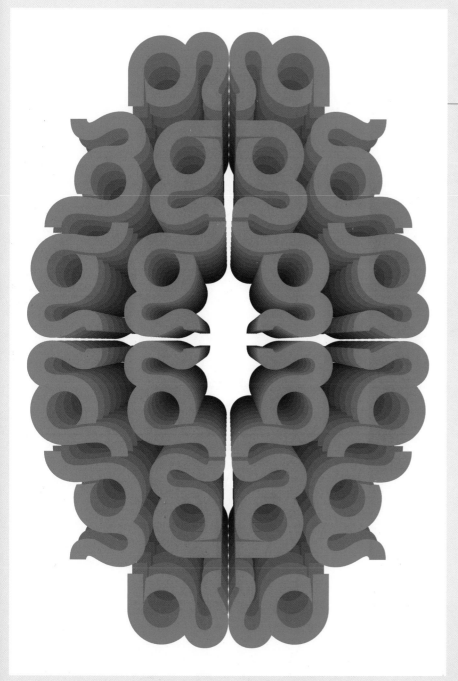

Aidan Nolan Design have used the "g" from the typeface Agostina to produce this decorative design based on imagery of the human brain.

Site-specific work at Casa FOA exhibition

by Yani Arabena and Guille Vizzari, Buenos Aires

This project was commissioned in 2009 by the Argentinean architecture studio PLAN, through Brasilia Prima, a graphic design studio based in Buenos Aires. It took place at Casa FOA, the interior and architectural design exhibition held every year in that city.

Yani Arabena and Guille Vizzari were asked to be part of a live intervention at PLAN, where artists developed site-specific work, responding to the environment. The concept involved wandering around the space, using the "table" as a place to share where people think, eat, work, play, and often create.

Yani and Guille developed an idea for five handmade book covers of different sizes and colors, which would contain large folded paper sheets incorporating illustrations and calligraphy.

They used a series of lettered phrases (decided prior to the event), which were cut in fluorescent orange self-adhesive vinyl, the kind often used for street signs.

These cut vinyl phrases were applied to the handmade covers and to other compositions including drawings, letters, and calligraphy. Other materials used in this process were markers, ink, calligraphy pens, paper-cut techniques, and papers of different textures and colors.

After the lettering, calligraphy, and other design work was completed, the resulting paper sheets were folded to fit within the book covers, resulting in five individual handmade books.

The space at PLAN where the site-specific work was undertaken.

One of the phrases cut out of a vinyl sheet.

The variety of materials, colors, and techniques used in this experimental project.

A decorated page.

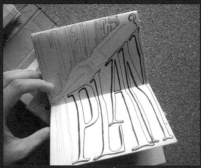

Folding one of the inserts ready for binding.

The five finished books, showing an example of the vinyl lettering applied to a cover.

BRUGAL
DESDE 1888
RON DOMINICANO

PRESENTS
JOE
CLAUSELL
JUNE 12

KLIKRECORDS

galaxy
BAR

**ATHENS HILTON/GALAXY BAR
DOORS OPEN AT 23:00**

Dimitris Kanellopoulos overprints
semitransparent inks to create this
strong typographic image.

Chapter 7 : Production considerations

Having completed your experimentation and research, you will need to draw together the various design elements toward the finished product. At various stages during this process you will have evaluated the work in terms of its effectiveness, visual appropriateness, and suitability for purpose. The final stage will be the preflight check to ensure that you have specified and supplied everything needed for production. Production factors include printing method, choice of stock, binding, paper size and format, size of screen and resolution, finishing processes, and software compatibility.

Evaluation

When you feel that your design is complete, it is important to stand back from it to ensure that what you have is what you want to go to production. In most cases, the work will be handed over to someone else, such as a printer or Web-developer, at this stage. Before this handover, it is a good idea to leave your design for a while and return to see it afresh. If you don't have time to do this, look at it in a mirror, reverse the image on the computer, or squint at it. This will give a new perspective and help you identify problems or anything that may need adjustment. As we have already discussed (see page 93), the text will need a final check. Mistakes in text are expensive—sometimes impossible—to remedy once the design has gone to production.

This design by Driv takes into account the space taken up by different languages.

TIP
If your design has to accommodate text translated into different languages, make sure that you have allowed for some flexibility in text length, as different languages take up different amounts of space.

!
Pitfall: Do not use spellcheck in place of a proofread, as it will miss all kinds of mistakes that would be obvious to the human eye. Beware automatic word substitution in word-processing packages, where a word may be replaced with something inappropriate without your knowledge. Check your settings!

An important aspect of the evaluation is checking that your design matches the original criteria and that all of the requirements of the brief have been met. Part of this process is ensuring that any technical requirements are achievable—for example, making sure that the stock you have chosen is suitable for the finish you envisage.

TIP
Always keep a reference copy of your work file exactly as it was when you handed it over for production (and keep copies of any relevant files and images).

Preflight

Preflight is a term borrowed from the safety checks on airplanes prior to takeoff and refers to preparation before publication. Many software packages include a preflight facility, but you will need to check that all your images are in the correct format and that you have specified the correct screen resolution in dots per inch (dpi) or pixels per inch (ppi). If you're working in a program that doesn't have a preflight check system, ensure that you have collected fonts, images, and any other items needed for output. Organization is important here: make sure that all items are identified correctly and you know where to find them (or that the software can find them).

TIP Check that the producer's systems are compatible with yours and that they will be able to read your files. This also applies to typefaces, which are not always the same across platforms.

Once you have prepared your files for production, it is worthwhile providing a printout of the finished work to the printer or other producer for reference and to prevent misunderstandings. Any special instructions, such as nonstandard finishes, stock, etc. should be clearly indicated on the printout.

Keep a photocopy of this mark-up for your own records in case the finished version is not as you intended. Usually the printer will supply a proof so that the designer and client can check for color and quality. Check typefaces carefully, to ensure that the printer has not used a different version. If a different version has been used, this may also affect text flow.

! **Pitfall:** Don't be tempted to make any adjustments to your design after the final proof has been produced. Printers charge extra for amendments post-proofing and it can cause delays in production.

The design process, using an iPad-sized dry whiteboard, for an app.

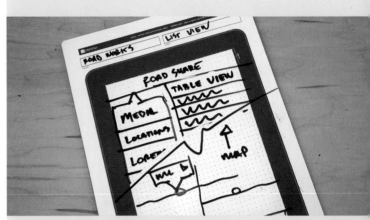

When working with a Web- or screen-based design developer it is important that they know what your intentions are for the final design. Screenshots or flowcharts are useful methods of specifying how the final design should appear. You can use screenshots (or pdfs) as reference for individual webpages, and a flowchart or wireframe (a diagram showing positioning of pages, information, and links) will provide a visual guide to the site's overall structure.

This close-up of a Yani Arabena design shows
the indentation made by printing calligraphic
letterforms onto textured stock.

Choice of stock

above: Music have used a heavy, textured stock to give presence to this design.

You will have considered stock at the outset of your design and it may be essential to the creative solution—for example, using a textured stock to give a rough, hand-produced feel to a printed design. There is a wide range of stock and substrates to consider when you are designing. A semi-opaque stock, for example, will give a sense of layering and will usually have a hard finish, which will give a sharp edge to any type printed on it; you could even print on the reverse of it, giving real depth and interest. Textured or absorbent stock may be used to create a more bespoke feel, but sometimes it can have an adverse effect on legibility and readability if the printing plate does not make good contact with the paper, causing areas of print to be missed. Typefaces with fine lines or serifs are particularly susceptible to such problems.

Weight

The overall feel of a printed publication may be affected by the weight of the stock used. A heavy or thick stock, for example, does not allow show-through of print from the reverse of the paper and can give a sense of quality, whereas a finer paper may suggest something more throwaway, especially if the printing on the reverse shows through. Difference in weight can be used as a navigational device; you might, for example, use a heavier stock for chapter openers so that readers can physically feel the divisions between chapters as they flick through a book. Paper weight is usually defined in pounds per ream (500 sheets) of uncut paper or in grams per square meter (gsm) and is an important consideration, particularly when designing for packaging as a certain weight may be required for strength and stability.

above: This booklet by Benjamin Koh takes advantage of the transparent quality of the paper so that the following page forms part of the cover design.

below: A section of the Robert Horne swatch book, Stardream, showing a range of paper and board with finishes such as metallic, pearlescent, and iridescent.

110 g/m² 1 sided	Onyx
120 g/m²	Anthracite
240 g/m²	Silver
285 g/m²	Coral
340 g/m²	Rose Quartz
Canneté	Kunzite
Orion	Amethyst
Seta	Punch
Crystal	Ruby
Diamond	Azalea
Quartz	Jupiter
Opal	Mars
Dolomite	Lagoon
Citrine	Aquamarine

TIP

Most paper companies will supply samples and color and weight swatches for their product range together with information on the qualities of the stock with reference to print and handling. It is worth keeping files of these samples for future reference and ideas generation.

left: John Christenson has modeled his Nuzzles®, interlinking letterforms in three dimensions, as stand-alone objects but they could work well if photographed and used in two-dimensional work.

center left: Kiss have used incised lettering to provide interest and texture in an architectural context.

below left: Maciej Mizer has used complex modeling and photomontage techniques to produce this simulated three-dimensional design, used on a T-shirt.

Finish

The finish on a stock can make a significant difference to a design. Coated papers with a less absorbent surface, for example, will reproduce small-sized or delicate typefaces well and are therefore suitable for fine detail. Uncoated stocks, in contrast, are often more absorbent and therefore more suitable for softer, less detailed work. If you want the best of both worlds, you can apply a coating to certain areas of uncoated stock, which gives scope for many creative design opportunities. Not all coated stock has a shiny, flat surface; some coatings may give a matte or textured finish. Coatings may be referred to in different terms, such as gloss, luster, satin, or silk. Other specialist print finishes include lamination and foil blocking. Lamination can protect stock and make it stronger, or it can be used as a spot effect—for example, to give a different finish to title type. This is also a way in which foil blocking is often used (see opposite, center right).

There is a view that glossy or coated stock is more damaging to the environment than uncoated stock, as the coating process uses more chemicals, but this is not always the case; check a stock's environmental credentials where possible. An uncoated, matte stock may appear more environmentally friendly than a coated one, but consider this in the context of the whole design, as your choice of typeface, color, and other factors will also affect perceptions.

There is now a huge range of materials that may be used for producing designs incorporating type. Modern production technology allows you to apply type to surfaces such as metals, plastics, and glass. It also provides opportunities to experiment with three-dimensional forms, such as store signage and architecture. These three-dimensional artifacts may be real objects that have been digitized and used in screen-based format, possibly even in virtual reality. Of course, three-dimensional effects may also be created from scratch digitally.

Type may also be put onto the surfaces of three-dimensional letterforms, perhaps as decoration or texture, to help interpretation. Further processes may be used to enhance

The cover for this brochure by The Consult has a high-gloss finish for impact and tactile quality.

A five-year skills strategy for the UK fashion and textiles sector
Skillfast-UK

above left: This is a sophisticated use of metallic ink on matte stock by The Consult.

above right: Ambush use foil block to give a sophisticated and luxurious look to this design.

right: Toko use simulated raised shapes to add texture and depth to this poster.

above: Marian Bantjes uses gold metallic ink on the lettering to illuminate this design.

below: Me Studio use photographs of people interacting with 3-D letterforms to create movement in this brochure design.

above: Fluid Design have incorporated embossing and die-cutting into this complex design, which attracts attention as well as giving a tactile quality.

below: To create impact, Martin Pyper has used laser-cut heavy white card in this pop-up design.

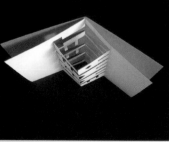

the design: finishes such as lamination, foil blocking, and varnishing may be applied to a variety of surfaces and offer creative opportunities as well as solutions to practical concerns such as waterproofing and durability.

UV (Ultra Violet) varnish, foil blocking, embossing, thermography (chemically raised ink surface), and flocking are examples of print finishes that can add value to your design. They can be used individually or in combination: for example, a foil-blocked and embossed detail may often be found on popular fiction books to attract attention when displayed for sale. Other finishes include fluorescent and metallic inks, debossing (see page 165), and die-cutting, which involves cutting out an area of a design. All these finishes add to the cost of production but offer opportunities for experimentation and communication and may be achieved within a variety of printing methods.

This is a poster that Hans Gremmen found at
a letterpress printer in Mexico City. Posters
for ephemeral events such as this "lucha
libre" (freestyle wrestling) competition have
to be produced quickly and cheaply: the
printer assembles the typefaces, logos, etc.
from items already available in his workshop.

Print processes

There are various specialist methods of producing type,
including lithography, letterpress, silkscreen, lino print,
woodblock, copperplate engraving, and etching—as well
as, of course, more basic methods such as potato prints
(see page 57). These processes are usually identified with
short print runs or fine print (limited edition), as they often
require skilled craftsmanship and specialist equipment;
you may find subtle differences between each print, which
conveys a sense of exclusivity. It is useful to understand
the idiosyncrasies of these processes, so that you can
exploit them to good effect. For example, letterpress
printing makes an indentation on the surface of the stock,
which produces a tactile quality (see below left).

Many of the effects associated with craft processes may be
replicated using software so that they can be incorporated
into design for both screen and commercial print. Offset
lithography is currently the most commonly used
commercial printing process. It is based on traditional
lithography in which the design is transferred to a plate
that takes up the printing ink and deposits it on the stock.

Inkjet and laser printing are commonplace in everyday
business and domestic situations. They are the printing
processes that you are most likely to use for proofing your
work or for printing one-offs or small runs at standard
sizes such as letter and ledger. These technologies, which
enable you to print more or less directly from software,
are now being adopted by some commercial printers.

This poster was produced on a Vandercook
letterpress by John Magnifico. Traditional
processes such as these can result in a
bespoke, hand-produced finish.

Printing can involve a certain amount of
trial and error—a fact of life that Hans
Gremmen recognizes and celebrates in this
silkscreen-printed poster, which is derived
from testprints that the designer found at
an Amsterdam printworks.

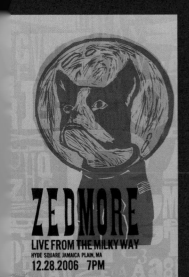

right: Daniel Muntean makes prints from a plywood woodblock—an experimental production technique that would not be suitable for mass production.

below: Marton Borzak used a UV varnish on a silk stock to emphasize the title of this book.

Kasper Pyndt created a typographic design to be printed on the floor and walls of a room. The design was printed in sections and a stencil was made from each of these in order to reproduce the design faithfully.

A process used by Szabó Balázs to produce embossed lettering. The letters are applied onto individual squares of metal using an acid-resist material. The squares are then etched in acid to leave the letterform proud of the rest of the square. The resulting forms are pressed into soft paper to produce embossed letterforms. This work experiments with production techniques, both in the making of the letterforms themselves and the way they are applied to the stock.

Artiva had this rubber stamp produced as part of a brand identity. This idea gives the client the flexibility to print their logotype wherever they like.

From his original lino prints (above), Andy
Cooke has been able to transfer this logo
design into a variety of digital and print
formats, including a webpage (below).

Color in production

Although it is possible to send your design direct to the commercial printer or producer, you will need to ensure that their software is compatible with yours and that what you send is what the final product will look like. It is disappointing to receive a finished piece of work from the printer only to discover, for example, that the contrast is much darker or lighter than it appeared on screen. It is normal practice, when designing for print, to make desktop printouts of your work to ensure that the printed piece resembles the screen version, but this is not a failsafe precaution. To get as close a color match as possible, calibrate your monitor and software with your desktop printer. However, it is not usually possible to perform this kind of calibration between your equipment and that of a commercial printer. Instead, you should receive a printer's proof, which will allow you to check, among other things, registration (see page 194) and color.

When designing on screen, colors are rendered in RGB (red, green, blue) format. However, RGB is not suitable for print work, so, for commercial printing, files will need to be converted to the four process colors: C (cyan), M (magenta), Y (yellow), and K (black) (CMYK). When matching specific colors, such as those used for corporate identities or brands, you would normally use a color-matching system, such as PANTONE® (see page 132). Digital versions of these color systems are often provided within design software.

The four-color process allows most colors to be reproduced by combining the four process colors in varying proportions. These are approximations of the real colors and, as stated before, if you want a particular color to be accurate, you would need to use an extra, specified color (see page 132). This only applies to conventional print methods: emerging print technologies, such as Print on Demand (POD), blend the colors through the technical process rather than breaking colors down into CMYK screens.

This screenshot shows a menu for the PANTONE® color-reference system provided within a graphics software package.

This packaging project by Aaron Alexander shows a creative use of misregistration.

Production for print

Although print- and screen-based projects may start out in a similar way, by the time they reach the production stage principles and processes differ dramatically. Key issues relating specifically to print-based production include registration and binding. Another thing to bear in mind is that the file formats for print will often be different from those for screen.

Registration and trapping

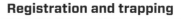

In color printing, each of the four process colors is printed on a separate plate. These plates need to be correctly aligned to ensure a clear and accurate reproduction. Correctly aligned plates are described as being "in register." You sometimes see examples of misaligned, or misregistered, printing in newspapers where one color is offset from another, creating a sort of ghost image. Misregistration can cause legibility problems, but can also be used creatively in a design. Deliberate misregistration, sometimes combined with different opacities of inks, can add depth and texture to a design. You can use software to reproduce such effects quite easily but, as with most effects, overuse may lessen the impact.

When two colors are misregistered, a gap appears where the colors meet (see left). Trapping is a method of compensating for this problem by printing small areas of overlapping color. Software programs usually add trapping automatically, but you should check your preferences in case you need to enable trapping or apply it manually.

Related to trapping, and often treated as the same, is knock out, which involves the first, or underlying, color being completely obliterated where the two colors overlap.

This letterform is misregistered with the background, leaving a white edge exposed.

Activity

Select a heavy typeface such as Souvenir (or a bold version of any typeface) and use this to produce a simple word of no more than five letters. Unless you want to create extra challenges, use letterforms such as "u" and "s" that do not have fully enclosed counters. Render this word in a fairly large point size (e.g. 150 point) on a piece of thin card (we used 180gsm smooth card). Cut out the letterforms to create a stencil. Place the stencil on a fresh sheet of paper and dab ink or paint through with a soft rag or brush. Remove the stencil and allow the ink or paint to dry before placing the stencil back on the paper but slightly offset from the first print. Repeat the inking process using a paint or ink in a different color or a different tint of the original color. You can repeat this as many times as you like to achieve a variety of effects.

Here a student cut out the stencil and inked through it, first in blue and then in red, using a large brush to produce a stippled effect.

The binding for this publication by Livius
Dietzel uses innovative techniques. The spine
of the book is exposed, showing the binding,
and Dietzel has used paper bags as pages,
embellished with embossing and die-cutting.

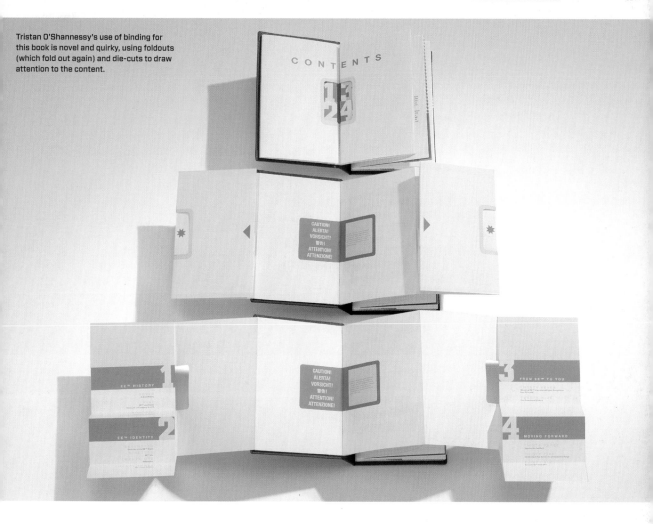

Tristan O'Shannessy's use of binding for
this book is novel and quirky, using foldouts
(which fold out again) and die-cuts to draw
attention to the content.

Binding

Although predominantly a practical consideration, the
binding of a book or any other multipage document can
also present opportunities for creative experiment. Various
methods are used for binding, the most common being
stitching, where the pages are stapled or stitched together
across the center; perfect binding, where the pages are
collected into sections and then glued across the spine;
and case binding, where pages are stitched in sections that
are then stitched together across the spine. Less common
bindings include stab binding, where the spine side of the
pages is pierced and then bound.

Decisions about binding are integral to the book as a
whole. For example, a tight binding can make the center of
the publication difficult to see, as the pages will not open
flat. The number of pages, thickness of stock, ergonomics,
size and format of the publication, and budget are all
factors that need to be taken into account when selecting
the binding. Large or thick books may need a hardback
binding to give them strength; such binding also carries
associations of quality and durability.

Design considerations relating to binding include the
width of margins, because a book with many pages may
need a wider inner margin to ensure that the content
toward the spine is visible and readable. Running text
or even large titles across the center of a publication
always presents the risk, even in expensive books, of
misalignment. Of course, such problems can create
opportunities for creative use of type and lettering.

Trapped in Suburbia disguise the spine using large letterforms with bright colors and shapes.

File formats for print

Unless you are providing a pdf (portable document format) where the typeface is embedded, you will need to make sure that the printer has access to the same typefaces as the ones used for your design.

When providing type as an object or image, such as a logotype, make sure that the resolution is appropriate to the print process. Software can be used to adjust resolution; the normal setting for high-quality publications is 300dpi.

Production for screen

There are certain key areas you will need to consider both when designing and handing over a Web or e-book project. For example, do you want your pages to resize automatically when users adjust the size of their browser window, or will page size be fixed? If you opt for a fluid layout, do you want all elements to be resizable? How will images and other graphics be affected? You also need to consider how your type design will react to users resizing text. Have you allowed enough vertical space for a larger type setting? How will text wrap at different size settings? Bear in mind that your choice of typeface for alterable text will generally be restricted to the standard typefaces supplied with users' operating systems.

When handing your design over to a developer, make sure that your files are well organized, as the developer may be less familiar with the software than you are. For example, if you have been working in Adobe Photoshop, clearly group and label the layers for each page. To ensure colors reproduce as you intend them to, provide a reference that gives the RGB values of key colors. As with print production, it is better to specify too much than too little.

TIP

The resolution for images used on screen is usually 72dpi; larger files may cause problems as they will take longer to load and will also take up more memory than they need to.

Legal issues and accessibility

It is important to be aware of copyright laws pertinent to the country or countries in which your work is to be published. This applies to content as well as typefaces and any images used.

It is also good practice to consider accessibility in your design. You will have seen statements on printed and screen-based design stating that there is a large-format version available for those with sight difficulties. Other accessibility issues include dyslexia and color blindness. Bear in mind that some countries have laws governing these issues.

Promotional brochure
by Mission Design, Norway

Mission Design's philosophy is based on simplicity. In this brochure
they explain their philosophy and the story behind the company.
The brochure includes seven case studies illustrating some of the
different challenges that clients have brought to the company.

Color matching and mixing for the cover and interior,
including the use of the PANTONE® matching system and
testing the custom metallic ink.

The proofing stage, where small adjustments are made to
hue and contrast.

The outside cover printed and ready for trimming and finishing.
Notice the crop marks to indicate folds and cuts. There are two
covers on a sheet to maximize the standard printer's paper size.

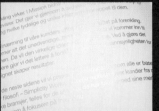

The finished brochure, which is 48 pages, perfect bound with
custom metallic ink and spot UV varnish.

Glossary

A2, A4, A5, etc.
ISO system of standardizing paper sizes, used in most countries except Canada and the United States. It begins with A0 (841 x 1189 mm). For each subsequent size the longer measurement is halved so A1 measures 594 x 841 mm. This continues to A10 (26 x 37 mm). The US system measures paper in inches; the standard letter size, equivalent to A4, is 8½ x 11 inches (216 x 279 mm). Other sizes in common use include legal (216 x 356 mm), executive (190 x 254 mm), and ledger/tabloid (279 x 432 mm).

Alignment
Whether text is vertically aligned left or right, justified, or centered (see also **ranged left/right**).

Appearing size
A term referring to the visual size of a typeface in relation to its **x-height**.

Ascender
The part of a letterform that projects above the **x-height** (see also **descender**).

Bar
The horizontal part of a letterform such as in the letter "e" or "A."

Bas-relief
Elements carved, sculpted in low relief, or in some way raised from a flat background.

Baseline
The invisible line at the base of a line of text on which the letters sit.

Bleed (in layout)
The term used when a layout element runs off the edge of a page or screen.

Body text or body type
Sections of text that are meant to be read, such as magazine articles or books (see also **copy**).

Bold
A letterform that is heavier/thicker in appearance than the ordinary/**Roman** form of the typeface.

Calligram
A section of text that is visually arranged to represent an idea or concept.

Calligraphy
Derived from the Greek for "beautiful writing," calligraphy is a traditional method of producing letterforms by hand.

Capitals/caps
Letterforms that are of equal height, such as ABC (see also **upper case**).

Centered
When text is **aligned** in a symmetrical format based on the center of the column.

CMYK
Acronym for the colors Cyan (C), Magenta (M), Yellow (Y), and Black (K) that make up the four-color printing process.

Color
The density, lightness, or darkness of a block of text.

Column
A block of text that is organized in a vertical structure on the page.

Column measure
The width of a column of text.

Condensed
A letterform that is narrower than the ordinary/**Roman** version of the typeface.

Copy
Sections of text that are meant to be read, such as magazine articles or books (see also **body text**).

Counters/counterforms
The spaces left between or within shapes and forms, as in "O," or partly enclosed, as in "E" (see also **negative space**).

Crosshead
See **subheading**.

Deboss
Where a design is stamped into the substrate, giving an indented effect.

Descender
The tail of a letterform that hangs below the **baseline** (see also **ascender**).

Die-cutting
Where a section of a design is cut out, often to reveal the material underneath, using a special metal form called a die.

Display typeface
A typeface that is designed to attract attention, usually used in larger sizes for small amounts of text such as titles and **headlines** rather than **body text**.

Double-page spread/dps
Two pages of a publication viewed adjacent to each other and in which the content is usually continuous.

dpi
Dots per inch—the closer together the dots, the more dots there are per inch, which results in higher quality.

Drop cap
When the first letter of a paragraph or section is larger than the **body text** and drops below the **baseline**.

Editorial
Refers to design that contains text for reading, such as newspapers, magazines, etc.

Em dash
A dash that is based on the width of the capital "M" in any size of type.

Emboss
Where a design is stamped into the reverse of the substrate, giving a raised or low-relief effect.

Emoticon
A symbol representing an emotion, such as :-) meaning a happy face.

En dash
A dash that is based on the width of the lowercase "n" or half an **em dash** in any size of type.

Expert set
A typeface that includes a set of letterforms/characters such as **ligatures** and fractions.

Family
A group of typefaces that are based on the same design, such as an **italic** and **bold** version of a **Roman** typeface.

Flatplan
A diagram of the pages of a publication laid flat, which is used by designers to help them work out how to arrange the various elements of the publication and provide an overview of the entire work.

Flowchart
A diagram showing the structure of a website or multimedia artifact.

Font
Originally the term (in Britain, fount) for a complete set, in one weight, style, and size, of characters such as letters, numbers, and punctuation marks for a particular typeface. It is now commonly used to refer to a **typeface** in one style or weight at any size.

Graphic elements/devices
Typographic items used in layout, such as arrows, exclamation marks, etc.

Grid
The underpinning structure for the page layout of most text-based design, usually made up of columns of text.

gsm
The weight of paper as represented in grams per square meter (gsm).

Hanging cap
When the first letter of a paragraph or section is larger than the **body text**, and sits outside the left-hand side of the column.

Headline
A typeface that is designed to attract attention, usually used in larger sizes for small amounts of text such as titles and headlines rather than body text (see also **body text**, **display typeface**).

Hierarchy
A system of prioritizing information to guide the reader or viewer.

Ideogram
Image or symbol used to represent a concept or action, conveying an abstract notion rather than a depiction of an object or person.

Imprint page
The page of a book that carries information about the author, publisher, publication date, copyright holders, etc.

Indent
To begin a line of text with a space, setting the line back slightly from the margin, such as at a new paragraph.

Initial cap
Signals a starting point to a section of text and helps draw the reader's eye as it stands out from the body text (variations include **drop caps** and **hanging caps**).

Italic
A letterform that is more sloped in appearance than the Roman form of the typeface. It derives from cursive writing and in some countries is called Kursiv or Cursive (see also **oblique**, **Roman**, **slant**).

Justified
When text is aligned vertically to both left and right sides of a column.

Kerning
Adjusting the space between a pair of letterforms (see also **letterspacing**). Referred to as kerned pairs.

202

Landsape format
Format where the longest dimension is horizontal (see also **portrait format**).

Leading or linespacing
The space between lines of type from one baseline to the next.

Legibility
Defines whether characters or groups of characters are understandable and may be easily distinguished.

Letterpress/movable type/metal type
A method of relief printing where the letterforms are raised in metal or wood type to form an area for the ink to be applied before printing.

Letterspacing
The space between letterforms (see also **kerning**, **tracking**).

Ligature
Where two letterforms are conjoined to form a distinctive shape.

Line length
The width of a line of text.

Lino print
A method of printmaking where the areas not to be printed are cut out from the surface of the lino.

Logo
Shortened from logotype, a design developed from a company's or institution's name or emblem that forms its visual and/or corporate identity.

Lower case
Letterforms that are not capitals, such as abc. Called this because when type was set by hand, two cases were used, the one holding capitals arranged higher (upper) than the other, which held the small letters (lower).

Measure
The length of a line of text. In grids, the width of a column is referred to as column measure.

Negative space
The spaces left between or within shapes and forms (see also **counters**).

Oblique
A letterform that is more slanted in appearance than the **Roman** form of the typeface (see also **italic**, **slant**).

Ornaments
A typeface or section of a typeface that comprises decorative items and symbols—also called dingbats, printer's flowers, or fleurons.

Outline
Where the contour of the letterform is outlined.

Pastiche
Reinterpreting historical styles and genres to support an idea.

pdf
Portable document format.

Pictogram
An image that represents an object or a person.

Points
A system for measuring a letterform.

Portrait format
Format where the longest dimension is vertical (see also **landscape format**).

ppi
Pixels per inch (ppi) is the measurement used for digital image resolution. Similar to **dpi**, the higher the ppi, the higher the resolution and quality.

Preflight
Checks and preparation before printing.

Pull quotes
A short section of text, a phrase, or quote, drawn out of an article in order to draw attention to the content.

Ranged left/right or ragged left/right
When a column of text is aligned vertically to the left- or right-hand side of the column.

Readability
How easy it is to read or understand a section of text.

Resolution: high, medium, low
The quality of the reproduction of an image, either for screen or print. High resolution means the image has higher definition and clarity for good-quality print-based work. Low resolution means an image will be less defined and therefore only suitable for use in screen-based work. In between is a range of resolutions suitable for different print processes. See also **dpi**, **ppi**.

Reversed out
Where text is lighter than the background.

RGB
Red Green Blue, the three colors that make up the digital color range.

Rivers
Formed when a series of large gaps between words appear above and below each other, linking together into a trickle-like pattern down the page.

Roman
The basic Latin letterform, ordinary, upright, and normal weight (for example not **bold** or **italic**).

Rules
Lines of various width, weight, and pattern.

Runaround
Where body text is wrapped around an item, also called text wrap.

Sans serif
Sans serif letterforms do not have small strokes at the ends of letterforms—hence "sans," which means "without" (see also **serif**).

Screen print/silk-screen print
A method of printing where ink is pushed through a fine mesh (screen), to which a stencil has been attached, onto the surface to form the image.

Screen resolution
The quality of an image, its resolution, in terms of the number of visible dots or pixels per inch.

Script
A typeface that mimics calligraphic or handwritten shapes. The letters usually have a connecting stroke.

Serif
Serif typefaces are based on Roman incised lettering, which features small strokes at the ends of letterforms (see also **sans serif**).

Show-through
In print design, where the image and/or text from the previous page is visible on the page being viewed.

Slab (block) serif
A **serif** that is pronounced and heavy in appearance.

Slant
A letterform that is more slanted in appearance than the **Roman** form of the typeface (see also **italic**, **oblique**).

Small caps
Smaller capital letterforms that are the size of the lowercase letters.

Spot color
Where a single (non-CMYK) color is used to highlight parts of a design.

Stem
The vertical strokes of a letterform.

Stock
Paper or other substrate.

Style sheet
Enables the designer to apply specific attributes, such as typeface or leading, to different sections of a document.

Subheading
A word or group of words that introduces a section of less importance than the title (see also **crosshead**, **hierarchy**).

Text linking/flowing/threading
The linkages between sections of text in a publication.

Thumbnails
Small sketches of design ideas.

Tracking
Adjusting the space between letterforms in a body of text (see also **letterspacing**).

Trapping
A method of compensating for the problem arising, in print, when a gap appears where two colors meet.

Typeface
A set of characters in a particular design.

Typogram
Type used as a visual way of encapsulating an idea.

Upper case
Term for capital letters such as ABC.

White space
The area of a design that does not contain any elements (the space may not necessarily be white).

Wireframe
A diagram showing positioning of pages, information, and links, usually used in website design.

Woodcuts/woodblocks
A method of printing where the image is produced by carving into the surface of a woodblock, leaving a raised area that is inked.

Word spacing
The gap between words in a block of text.

x-height
The distance from the top of a lowercase "x" to its base.

Some further reading

Austin, Tricia and Richard Doust. *New Media Design*, Laurence King Publishing, 2007

Baines, Phil and Andrew Haslam. *Type & Typography*, second edition, Laurence King Publishing, 2005

Craig, James. *Designing with Type: The Essential Guide to Typography,* fifth edition, Watson-Guptill Publications, 2006

Cranford Teague, Jason. *Fluid Web Typography,* New Riders, 2009

Dodd, Robin. *From Gutenberg to OpenType: An Illustrated History of Type from the Earliest Letterforms to the Latest Digital Fonts*, Ilex, 2006

Elam, Kimberly. *Grid systems: Principles of Organizing Type*, Princeton Architectural Press, 2004

Garfield, Simon. *Just My Type: A Book about Fonts*, Profile Books, 2011

Gatter, Mark. *Production for Print*, Laurence King Publishing, 2010

Haslam, Andrew. *Book Design*, Laurence King Publishing, 2006

Haslam, Andrew. *Lettering: A Reference Manual of Techniques*, Laurence King Publishing, 2011

Heller, Steven and Lita Talarico. *Graphic: Inside the Sketchbooks of the World's Great Graphic Designers,* Thames & Hudson, 2010

Jaspert, W.P., W. Turner-Berry, and A.F. Johnson. *Encyclopaedia of Typefaces*, 55th anniversary edition, Cassell Illustrated, 2009

Jury, David, *Letterpress: The Allure of the Handmade,* second edition, Rotovision, 2011

Kane, John. *A Type Primer*, second edition, Pearson Prentice Hall, 2011

Loxley, Simon. *Type: The Secret History of Letters,* I.B. Tauris, 2006

Lupton, Ellen. *Thinking with Type*, second edition, Princeton Architectural Press, 2010

Marshall, Lindsey and Lester Meachem. *How To Use Images*, Laurence King Publishing, 2010

Meggs, Philip B. and Alison W. Purvis. *Meggs' History of Graphic Design,* fourth edition, John Wiley & Sons, 2006

Morley, Simon. *Writing On The Wall: Word and Image in Modern Art*, Thames & Hudson, 2007

O'Donnell, Timothy. *Sketchbook: Conceptual Drawings from the World's Most Influential Designers*, Rockport, 2009

Rivers, Charlotte. *Handmade Type Workshop: Techniques for Creating Original Characters and Digital Fonts*, Thames & Hudson, 2011

Squire, Victoria. *Getting it Right with Type: the Dos and Don'ts of Typography*, Laurence King Publishing, 2006

Stawinski, Gregor. *Retro Fonts*, Laurence King Publishing, 2010

Vollauschek, Tomi and Agathe Jacquillat. *The 3D Type Book*, Laurence King Publishing, 2011

Willen, Bruce and Nolen Strals. *Lettering and Type: Creating Letters and Designing Typefaces,* Princeton Architectural Press, 2009

Zappaterra, Yolande. *Editorial Design,* Laurence King Publishing, 2007

Websites

Design associations and societies

ATypI (Association Typographique Internationale)
http://www.atypi.org/

British Design & Art Direction
http://www.dandad.org/

International Society of Typographic Designers
http://www.istd.org.uk/

The Society of Typographic Aficionados (SOTA)
http://www.typesociety.org/

Type Directors Club
http://www.tdc.org/

History and libraries

Design is History
http://www.designishistory.com/

The Library of Congress
http://www.loc.gov

St Bride Library
http://www.stbride.org/

Six Revisions: useful information for Web developers and designers
http://sixrevisions.com/web_design/a-basic-look-at-typography-in-web-design/

Fonts to buy

Emigre
http://www.emigre.com/

Type Art (novelty and graphic fonts)
http://www.typeart.com

Graphic design magazines

http://baselinemagazine.com

http://www.creativereview.co.uk

http://www.eyemagazine.com

Typography forums

http://www.planet-typography.com

http://typography.net/

http://www.typophile.com

http://welovetypography.com/

Technical and legal

http://www.adobe.com

Type Right (good information on typefaces as intellectual property)
http://www.typeright.org

The Unicode Consortium
http://www.unicode.org

Index

Picture credits

t = top, b = bottom, c = center, l = left, r = right

Introduction

7: Artwork and Design: Marian Bantjes. Client: The Grateful Palate/R Wines 2008 / 8 t: HVD Fonts / 8 b: Carol Cooper (carolcooper9@ tiscali.co.uk) / 9 tl: Bibliothèque de L'Arsenal, Paris, France/The Bridgeman Art Library / 9 tr: AKG Images / 9 cr: Fotolia.com / 9 br: Fotolia.com / 10 t: Barbara Brownie, *Oi*, 2009 / 10 bl: Hand & Eye Letterpress / 10 br: Society of Revisionist Typographers (SORT) Theo Wang and Tom Boulton / 11 t: Lester Meachem / 11 b: Christopher Wakeling at his Typographic Design Unit / 12 t: Co-creators: Dan Marino and Joe Mann / 12 bl: Fotolia.com / 12 br: Design by Artiva Design—Daniele De Batté/Davide Sossi. www.designq.co.uk / 13: Design and photography by Steven Acres. Content of the book based on lectures by SCAD Professor Zoran Belic / 14 t: Identity designed by Damien Poulain and Anthony Burrill / 14 b: Graphic design, calligraphy, and photo by Jordan Jelev, The Labelmaker, 2008. www.epixs.eu. Print: rotoprint-bg.com / 15 tl: © Jennifer Vejvoda/iStockphoto / 15 tr: Palete Industries (Samuel Ho, Ian Campana, Nathan Tremblay) / 15 bl: © Frank van den Bergh/ iStockphoto / 15 br: Private Collection/Peter Newark Military Pictures/The Bridgeman Art Library / 16 tl: Jamie Portch / 16 tr: Vaarwel Bar/Client: AKV St. Joost. www.akvstjoost.nl/ Year: 2007/Silkscreen printed/Design: Attak / 16 bl, bc, br: British Heart Foundation / 17 tl: Petar Pavlov / 17 cl: Creative Director: Vince Frost. Design Director: Carlo Giannasca / 17 cr: Design: Fons Hickmann m23. Photography: Fons Hickmann. Client: Bavarian State Opera, Munich / 17 br: Eurico Sá Fernandes www. eurico.ws / 18: Development of the new alphabet for the communication of the 5th Berlin Biennale / 19 tl, tr: Concept, programming and design by Andreas Müller, Nanika / 19 bl, br: Full Flash website portfolio. Author Michal Tilsch AKA Comandeer.

Chapter 1

20: by courtesy of Sebastian Carter / 22: Lindsey Marshall / 23 t: *The Times*/CHI & Partners / 23 bl: Design and illustration: Charlie Calderin. Design Agency: Doink, Inc. Coral Gables, FL, USA. www.doinkdesign.com. Client: Avanti Fine Men's Clothing / 23 br: Graphic Design: Artiva Design—Daniele De Batté/Davide Sossi / 24 tl: Eurico Sá Fernandes www.eurico.ws / 24 tr: Atelier Martino&Jaña / 24 br: Art Direction: Hannes von Döhren (www.hvdfonts.de), Livius F. Dietzel (www.liviusdietzel.de/) / 25 tl: InsaneFacilities, Jarek Berecki / 25 tr: Eva Blanes/www.evablanes.com / 25 cl: Ross Elliott / 25 cr: Typeface by Ale Paul. Photography by Gonzalo Aguilar / 25 b: Telekinesis Music. Photo by Jenny Jimenez / 26: Poster for "Just for Your Eyes Cinema Festival" 2008. A students' festival in Crete. Design: Dimitris Kanellopoulos, www.b-positiv. gr / 27 tl: Ragnar Freyr—www.ragnarfreyr.com / 27 tr: Art Direction: Astrid Stavro. Graphic Design: Studio Astrid Stavro / 27 bl: Defence Force Recruiting, Sydney / 27 br: Jennifer Morla poster with Kelsey Allen dropcap / 28: Lindsey Marshall. Photo: John Seth Marshall / 29: Typography, design, and art direction by Amirali Ghasemi. Illustration by Iman Raad / 30: Art Direction: Hannes von Döhren (www. hvdfonts.de), Livius F. Dietzel (www. liviusdietzel.de/) / 31: Blake Allen Design / 32 l: Type specimen created for the typeface Deibi, created by Joan Ramon Pastor / 32 r: Johan Skybäck / 33: Lindsey Marshall / 34 tl: "Sport Design" poster, 2004. Client: Museum of Design, Zurich. Design: Martin Woodtli. / 34 bl, br: "Sport Design" invitation card, 2004. Client: Museum of Design, Zurich. Design: Martin Woodtli. / 34 tr, cr: Project: Font for a design exhibition. Title: "Play." Client: Museum of Design, Zurich. Design: Martin Woodtli. / 35: Lindsey Marshall / 36 t: Lester Meachem / 36 b: Design and Animation by Joost Korngold. Music by Richard Emmet / 37 all: Lindsey Marshall / 38: Typography and Art Direction Andrew Townsend @ un.titled. Photograph Simon Congdon @ un.titled. Layout and design ADA and un:titled / 39 t: This commemorative stamp was produced in 2005 for the Swiss Post to celebrate 100 years of Einstein's discovery of the theory of relativity in Bern in 1905, while the scientist was living in Switzerland. The designer Jean-Benoît Lévy combined the sign "=" in the letter "E," allowing the formula to be more condensed / 39 b: Art Director: Maja Bagić Barić (KO:KE kreativna farma) / 40–41: Design: Martin Woodtli, CH. Title: "9 Evenings Reconsidered: Art, Theater, and Engineering." Client: Museum of Design Zurich. Declaration: 90.5 x 128 cm, silkscreening, four colors, A5, offset, four colors. Photo by Peter Moore © Estate of Peter Moore/ VAGA, NYC.

Chapter 2

42: Eva Blanes/www.evablanes.com / 44 t: Photos: Vava Ribeiro / 44 b: Design: Ludovic Balland, Typography Cabinet, Basel / 45 t, c: Lindsey Marshall / 45 b: Alex Cornell / 46 t: Ravi Vora, Creative Director/Designer. Agency: Ciplex.com / 46 bl: Client: Fluff SB/Adrien Bullard Interview in Fluff SB. Design: Vijf890 Ontwerpers www.vijf890.nl / 46 br: Shawn Strub: Vocal/lyric / 47 tl: Sara Falcón, Raiko Moeller, Stefan Kuzajand, Cláudia Pereira / 47 tr: Lindsey Marshall / 47 bl: Graphic Design: Artiva Design—Daniele De Batté/Davide Sossi / 47 br: Saks packaging by Pentagram Design / 48 tl: Design Atelier Martino&Jaña + Illustration Marcelo Oliveira / 48 c, bl, br: Lindsey Marshall / 49 t, br: Lindsey Marshall / 49 bl: John Ross ©V&A Images/Victoria and Albert Museum, London / 50 t: Editorial design for the Basel-based Imagine Festival against Racism. Art direction and design: Andreas Hidber, accent graphe. / 50 b: Lindsey Marshall / 51 t: Concept, layout, and typesetting: Christina Hackenschuh, Stuttgart, Germany / 51 b: Andrea Bussetti. Interior design product shot: Kelly Branan / 52: Creative Director: Vince Frost, Design Director: Ant Donovan, Design: Serhat Ferat, Digital Animator: Kat Clark / 53 tl, tr: Packaging and design are original. The written copy is derived from the original movie resources/ DVD/Wikipedia / 53 b: Bee Groupe / 54: Art Direction and Design Daniele de Batté and Davide Sossi (Artiva Design). Copywriter Irina Gandini. Client King-Dome / 55 t: Rawterdam, Côme de Bouchony, 2006 / 55 b: Lindsey Marshall. Photo: J S Marshall / 56 t: "The Price of Peace," March 2008. Layout and design by Lauren Burke. Letterpress title in collaboration with Nathan Haas. Content written by Pervenia P. Brown, "Blood Diamonds." World Press, 2005 / 56 b: Ryan Spacey, 2008. www.ryanspacey.com / 57 all: Lindsey Marshall and Lester Meachem / 58 t: Atelier Martino&Jaña / 58 b: Dan Alexander & Co., Avi Shaham / 59: Staynice/ AKV St. Joost. www.akvstjoost.nl / 60: Creative Director Alex Atkinson. Designer John-Paul Warner / 61 t, c: Lindsey Marshall / 61 b: Typeface, design, and layout by KalleGraphics / 62 t: Lindsey Marshall / 62 b: Mina Arko / 63 tl, br: Lester Meachem / 64 t: Design Studio: Default Bangkok www.defaultbkk.org. Designer: Akarit Leeyavanich / 64 b: Illustration and design concept by Inksurge. Ramon E.S. Lerma, Yael Buencamino, Joel de Leon, Ian Carlo Juacian of Ateneo Art Gallery / 65: Modefabriek 2010 photography by Philippe Vogelenzang @ Unit C.M.A. Lettering by Job Wouters/Letman. Model: Saskia de Brauw. Hair/make-up: Judith Neyens for Chanel @ NCL Representation / 66: Jordi Serra Santano / 67 tl: Mina Arko / 67 bl: Attila Horvath—designer, typographer / 67 br: Monotype. Photo by John Seth Marshall / 68: Lindsey Marshall / 69: Livory is a serif type family of four fonts including small caps, ligatures, and ornaments. It was designed by Hannes von Döhren and Livius Dietzel between 2005 and 2010 / 70: Title: *Amnesty Aktion* Magazine. Client: Amnesty International. Design: Fons Hickmann m23.

Chapter 3

72: Michael Horsham @ Tomato for Museion, Museum of Contemporary Art, Bolzano, Italy / 74: "Typographic Map of Wales" produced by Hannah Rummery while attending the BA Hons Graphic Design Course at Sheffield Hallam University. The artwork was produced in response to a YCN project brief set by Visit Wales as part of the final year of study. January 2009 / 75: Between Two Waters. A project to encourage reflection and speculation about water. To draw two looks for the same drop, one vision from science, the other from consciousness. (Cyan = Science, Magenta = Consciousness) It isn't a fight between egos, but an essay of opinions, hypothesis, and discovery about water and its environment / 76: Sherrie Thai, ShaireProductions.com / 77: Lindsey Marshall. Photo: John Seth Marshall. Z Brand tag used with permission / 78: Agency: Boondoggle (www.boondoggle.eu). AD + Design: Petra Sell (www.zappness.net). Development: Hans Dreesen, Dirk Weckx / 79: Creative Direction: Claire Dawson, Fidel Peña. Design: Brian Banton, Clea Forkert. Mattering Maps Illustration: Emmanuel Polanco. *Rotman* magazine designed by Underline Studio, Toronto, Canada / 80 tl: Todd Moy/Viget Labs / 80 tr: Photo by Luis Mendo / 80 b: Agency: Fluid Studio. Designer: Kevin Perry. Client: The Gallivan Center / 81 tl, bl: Lindsey Marshall / 81 br: Lindsey Marshall. Photo: John Seth Marshall / 82: Mariela Dommarer, Keila Hötzel, Werner Hötzel—Designers and Art Direction / 83 t: Li Mei Tan / 83 b: Fluid / 84 t: A spread from the "Numberless" book; part of a survey/thesis conducted by Rob Ferrell while studying Graphic Design at the Maryland College of Art / 84 b: Annabelle Fiset, made in collaboration with Toast studio / 85: 841 x 1088mm, uncoated paper. Designed by Kimoon Kim (Director of a graphic design studio mykc). Texts from *Animal Farm*, George Orwell / 86: Design: Tomato Košir. Client: Modrijan založba, d. o. o. Editor: Julija Uršič. Printed by: Grafika Soča. Papers used: inside: Maestro Print 120 g/m2, cover: Hello 150 g/ m2 / 87 t: Moa Nordahl. Tiles by Hanna Werning / 87 b: Creative direction, design, and animation by Brent Barson. Music by Micah Dahl Anderson. Actor: John Troutman / 88 t: Creative Director Roman Krikheli. Designers Dmitry Rybalkin, Ilya Lovtsov, Ivan Popov / 88 c: Attak Powergestaltung. Peter Korsman and Casper Herselman for *Reload* magazine/Bold Publishing 2007 / 88 b: Joe Shepter: Text. Jimmy Chen: Design / 89 t: Art Direction and Design: Alexander Blücher, Photography: Blücher, Dmitry Zhuravlev / 89 b: Jiansheng Cui. A personal project for an MA course on experimental typography / 90 tl: Lindsey Marshall / 90 tr: Creative direction Siniša Sudar and Maro Pitarević. Art director and design—Siniša Sudar, Copywriting—Maro Pitarevic. Video: Tomica Kaćunić, Sound: Hrvoje Štefotić / 90 bl: Art Direction: Domestika / 90 br: Title: Bahia de todos os santos. Client: ifa Gallery. Design: Fons Hickmann m23 / 91: Commissioned by: M-Net, South Africa. Art Director: Matthew Stephen. Agency: Orijin (www.orijin.co.za) / 92 t: Type Design: Peter Crnokrak / 92 bl: Francis Fukuyama, *State Building*, Estonian cover. Cover artwork and design by Dan Mikkin, Brand Manual Ltd. Published by Tänapäev, Tallinn, Estonia 2006 / 92 br: Daniil Harms, *Ootamatu Jooming*, Estonian cover. Cover artwork and design by Dan Mikkin, Brand Manual Ltd. Published by Tänapäev, Tallinn, Estonia 2006 / 93: Trendsetter type: Paul Hollingworth. www.ph-graphic.co.uk / 94–95: Designed by Federico Galvani. Photographed by Federico Padovani with the support of Jamie N Kim, Mo Manager, and Wieden+Kennedy.

Chapter 4

96: Craig Redman / 98 t: Client: Booktrust / 98 b: Type Design: StudioOscar.com. Photo: Chris Coulson (www.christhecreative.com) at (Agency) WWAV Rapp Collins / 99: Hila Ben-Navat / 100: Typeface and poster designed by Áron Jancsó, 2009 / 101 l: Angelos Ntinas (Art Director). Unusual Design Group / 101 tr: © 2009 Poordesigners / 101 br: Mike Walsh, Futuretainment (www. mike-walsh.com)/Frost Design / 102 t: Peter Kowalski, wordboner.com / 102 b: Canthaid / 103 l: Poster was created in the type workshop tpobrda, Mentor: Prof. Lucijan Bratuš, Tomato Košir. Academy of Fine Arts and Design, Ljubljana, Slovenija / 103 r: Viento by Ale Paul & Angel Koziupa for Sudtipos / 104: Design by Jason Munn. Insound, New York. / 105 t: Publisher: Magma Brand Design GmbH & Co. KG. Editors in Chief: Lars Harmsen, Uli Weiss. Art Direction: Flo Gaertner, Lars Harmsen. Graphic Design: Julia Kahl. Managing Editor: Julia Kahl. Editors: Flo Gaertner, Lars Harmsen, Julia Kahl / 105 b: Harry Siefert, ARTFATALE—book, *You Look For Design*, www. youlookfor.us / 106: Design: Robin Uleman (www.robinuleman.nl) / 107 l: Design by alicetait.com. Headline / 107 r: Design proposal for Orion books. Design and Photography: Ami Smithson at cabinlondon. co.uk / 108 tl: Michal Bialogrzywy / 108 r: Áron Jancsó, 2008 / 108 bl: Type Factory by Huda Abdul Aziz (2009) / 109: Name: Fons Hickmann, Company: Fons Hickmann m23, Client: Laboratory for Social and Aesthetical Development, Title: Clothing Collection, Design: Fons Hickmann / 110 l: Project by: Designers Against Human Rights Abuse. Client: Tibet Relief Fund. Design/Typography: Stefan Gandl (NeuBauBerlin). Creative Director: Rishi Sodha (2Creatives) / 110 bl: Design by Corey Holmes / 110 br: Heye & Partner GmbH. Süddeutsche Zeitung Magazin / 111 t: Graphic Design and typography by kissmiklos (Miklos Kiss) / 111 b: Art Direction and Design: Michael McDonald. Programming: Ransom Weaver, Michael McDonald. Photography: Zave Smith / 112 t: © 2011 The Absolut Company AB / 112 b: Wellcome Images / 113: Pentagram Design Ltd. / 114 tl: Lindsey Marshall / 114 cl: Lindsey Marshall and Lester Meachem / 114 tr: Veronica Solomon, Art Director and Graphic Artist. Work is inspired by and meant as a tribute to early computer games (8-bit games) / 114 bc: Positive Quotes for Diary (this is me and this is mine)—Houri Nouri / 114 br: Designed by Malcolm Grear Designers, 1983 / 115 t: Photography: Proces 15 / 115 b: Studio Blue—Design firm; Kathy Fredrickson—Creative Direction; Garrett Niksch—Design and Illustration; Lauren Boegen—Project Management / 116 tr, cr: Opal Typefamily designed by Hannes von Döhren, 2008. More info: www.hvdfonts.com / 116 bl: Illustration/Art Direction—Si Scott Studio. Art Direction—Steve Banks www. paper-scissor-stone.co.uk / 116 br: MAF thesis project between Ashely Ciecka and Michael Jeter / 117 t: Tom Tor Studio. Website: www. tomtor.com. Email: hello@tomtor.com. Creative Director: Tom Tor. Design and Illustration: Tom Tor. Animation: Miguel Vasquez. Programmer: Jason Hickner / 117 b: Site design for Zachte G Evnt, commissioned by Zachte G/Betawerk. Art direction and design by Tom Bogman together with Maarten Mulders and Thuy Tran © 2009—FARB / 118-119: André Apel—Design and Direction; Jan Schöttler—Ideas and Concept; Kim Hensler—Website Design and Programming; Thomas Wimmer—Filming and Editing.

Chapter 5

120: Áron Jancsó, 2008 / 122 l: Lester Meachem / 122 r: Stefan Lucut and Ravi Vasavan / 123 l: Reuben Rosh aka Doubler / 123 r: i-creativ Studio http://i-creativ.net / 124 tl: Trapped in Suburbia / 124 tr: ATTAK Powergestaltung © 2010 Client: Greytones / 124 b: Designer: Danis Sie / 125 t: Autopromotional material for Playful's website / 125 b: Direction and Design: Andrey Nepomnyaschev. Sound: HECQ / 126 t: Côme de Bouchony / 126 cl: © Ophelia Chong / opheliachong.org / 126 bl: Ambush / 126 br: Oguzhan Ocalan, Gravitart Design Studio / 127 t: © Poordesigners 2007 / 127 b: Designed by Erretres. 15 Años de Fotografía Española

Contemporánea. Colección Alcobendas / 128 t: www.ilsh.se, nils@ilsh.se / 128 b: Bombastudio, A Magazine/Brutalism issue. Project management: Jan Bielak, Ewa Pawluczuk / 129 l: Poster for "De Veenfabriek"/Risograph print, 2009. In cooperation with Yvo Sprey / 129 r: Choeur Faller/Jacques-Henri Addor. Graphic Designer: Jean-Benoît Lévy. Photo: Stephen Collyer / 130: Martin Woodtli, martin@woodt.li / 131: Artwork, Web design and programming by Alien Art Agency. Content by Rip Curl Europe / 132 t: Zion Graphics / 132 b: Graphic Design by Andreas Hidber, accent graphe / 133 l: Image courtesy of Centro Cultural Vila Flor—Guimarães (Portugal) and created by Atelier Martino&Jaña. Design: Atelier Martino&Jaña and Claudia Santos / 133 r: Jason Munn / 134: Lester Meachem / 135 t: Melvin Galapon / 135 b: Directors: Blac Ionica. Designers: Blac Ionica. Agency: Devilfish. Creative Director: Matt Cole. Client: Food Network. Sound: Blac Ionica / 136 t: Design: Jonathan Arundel. www. jonathanarundel.co.uk. Victoria and Albert Museum / 136 b: © Ellen Zhao/BURO-GDS. Photo: Guillaume Boyard / 137 t: Designed by David Hitner and Guy Marshall / 137 b: Tobias Battenberg, 2007 / 138 t: Sound: Kungen and Hertigen, Client: MTV Denmark, Creative/Animation/Grading: Thank You APS / 138 b: Jeffrey Shaw / 139: Directors: Jackson & Karinja. Client: Freebord / 140: Creative direction, design, and animation by Brent Barson. Music by Micah Dahl Anderson. Actor: Jon Troutman / 141: Cortex—Identity. Julien Breton aka Kaalam. Light calligraphy, no digital manipulation—www.kaalam.com / 142: Permanent light installation by Sanjeev Shankar. www.sanjeevshankar.com. Photograph by Don Hildred / 143: Design by Yorgo Tloupas. Charly Leborgne/blackcrows / 144 t, b: The Chase. Manchester Evening News / 145 t: Beach calligraphy by Andrew van der Merwe, Noordhoek Beach, Cape Town / 145 b: Livius Dietzel. Album artwork for the German neopostmodern band "Die Reiter" about slowly fading love / 146 l: Sydney Dance Company. Frost Design/Vince Frost. Designer Caroline Cox. Illustrator Kelvin Robertson / 146 b: Lindsey Marshall / 147 tl, tr: Moshik Nadav / 147 bl, br: Pentagram Design Ltd. / 148-149: Thomas Pavitte.

Chapter 6

150: Arturo Pérez Zúñiga a.k.a. colorless / 152 tl, tr: Ralph Burkhardt, Daniel Hauke / 152 b: Dario Verrengia. A TYPE OF—Universal Declaration of Human Rights. www. cargocollective.com/darioverrengia / 153 t: Patrick Holmes/The Consult Design Ltd. / 153 b: Lee Stokes / 154: Design and typography: Alastair Stephens. Copy: Chris Arnold. Creative Directors: Victoria Gallardo and Chris Arnold / 155 tl: Ragnar Freyr—www. ragnarfreyr.com / 155 tr: Petar Pavlov / 155 br: Joan Ot Comellas / 156 t: Lindsey Marshall / 156 b: Name: Fons Hickmann m23, Company: Fons Hickmann m23, Title: Mercedes-Benz Museum, Design: Fons Hickmann m23/HG Merz, Photography: Markus Buesges / 157 t: Design Partner: Rick Valicenti/3st. Designer and photographer: Bud Rodecker/3st. Architect: Studio/Gang Architects. Columbia College Chicago / 157 bl: Lindsey Marshall /

157 br: Frederico Gontijo/Tiago Pereira/Tomas Faria / 158 tl: Piel Script © Ale Paul, Sudtipos www.sudtipos.com / 158 tr: Lindsey Marshall. Photo by John Seth Marshall / 158 b: Ivan Khmelevsky / 159 l: Lindsey Marshall / 159 b: © 2011 Jim Lind www.jimlind.com / 160: Felix Vorreiter, www.fel-x.com / 161: The Calligraphic World of Mi Fu's Art. National Palace Museum Taiwan, Republic of China / 162: Job Wouters. Lettering for Audi. Design Miami 2009, in cooperation with Mutabor (GE) / 163 t: Etching printer, Terry Fernandez, © www.lachocolaterie.li, Switzerland / 163 c: Image © Designer Bookbinders. Photographer Sussie Ahlburg / 163 br: Nouvelle Vague flyer by Eurico Sá Fernandes. www.eurico.ws, hi@eurico.ws / 164 t: Image courtesy of the artist: Kelly Mark and Diaz Contemporary (Toronto) / 164 cl: Barbara Brownie, Untitled Letter Objects, 2009 / 164 cr: Lego table designed and constructed by abgc architecture and design. Photo by Andrew Brady and Gearóid Carvill / 164 b: Boy Bastiaens: Art Direction and Design. Albert Kiefer: Design and Animation / 165 t: Mission Design / 165 b: Work produced in response to a university brief based around the association for dogs, Aaron Alexander / 166 tl: ALPHABET II—Roll-up, pop-out poster 30 x 20 ins, designed by Ron King and printed on pure rag paper at Circle Press, London 1999. www. circlepress.com / 166 tr: Daniel Taubert. www. danieltaubert.de, post@danieltaubert.de / 166 b: Urban Carpet: Orange, 2009 (detail), by Marcella Campa and Stefano Avesani. Embroidery on canvas, 190 x 190 cm. Web: instanthutong.com / 167 t: Kerve Creative, Bath. www.kerve.co.uk / 167 c: Design and printing by Alejandra Román (personal project for college) / 167 b: John Seth Marshall / 168 t: Lindsey Marshall / 168 b: Design: Fons Hickmann m23/HG Merz Architects. Client: Mercedes-Benz Museum. © Daimler AG / 169 t: Matthew Forrester / 169 b: Technical assistance: Ludvík Pelouch. Photo: Tereza Trautmanová / 170 t: Brill (neon sign). Design: StudioOscar.com. Brill, 27 Exmouth Market, London EC1 / 170 cl: Faber Film Image © Stewart Walker and Alastair Griffiths / 170 bl: Poster and card for design exhibition, titled "True Light." Museum of Design, Zurich. 90.5 x 128 cm, silkscreen, four colors / 170 br: Created by Camilo Rojas / 171 t: Agency Euro RSCG Lisboa. Advertiser: Optimus Kanguru. Product: Colored pens. Category: Mobile broadband. Client: Hugo Figueiredo, Pedro Moreira da Silva, Isabel Costa, Carolina Almeida. Human Typography: Amandine Alessandra. Creative Direction: Sara Ferreira and José Vieira. Art Direction: Francisco Chatimsky. Copywriter: André Águas. Web: Rui Lourenço, Ricardo Silva, and Pedro Portugal / 171 cr: Brian Banton / 171 cr: Lindsey Marshall / 171 b: Paper Engineer/Design: Benja Harney www.paperform.com.au, Art Direction: Rowena New / 172 t: Studio Zim & Zou / 172 b: Anderson—Trigger/Harney—Paperform. Shigeru Ban and Toland Architectural Design Partners University of Sydney document. All images © Trigger / 173 t: Concept and Design: Rick Valicenti/3st / 173 b: Johnie Clayton: Art Director. Christian Hogue: Director. Maitri Boonkijrungpaisa: Animation lead. Client: Nokia. Design Agency: Lunch Communications.

Production Company: Lost In Space / 174 t: Dario Verrengia. A TYPE OF—Universal Declaration of Human Rights. www. cargocollective.com/darioverrengia / 174 bl: Fitzwilliam Museum, University of Cambridge, UK/The Bridgeman Art Library / 174 br: Illustration, typography, and graphic design by Paul Grabowski www.paulgrabowski.com / 175: Aidan Nolan and A.N.D. Studio / 176-177: Yanina Arabena. Buenos Aires, Argentina www.yaniarabena.com.ar, hola@yaniarabena. com/Guillermo Vizzari. Buenos Aires, Argentina. www.behance.net/yaniguille, guillevizzari@gmail.com.

Chapter 7

178: Client: Klik Records © Poordesigners 2009 / 180: Art Director: Peter Zheng, Designer: Driv Loo, Photographer: Tony Chan. Wieden and Kennedy Advertising Inc. (WK SH) / 181 t, b: uistencils.com / 182: Calligraphy by Yanina Arabena, Buenos Aires, Argentina. www. yaniarabena.com.ar, hola@yaniarabena.com. ar. Printed in letterpress by Federico Cimatti (Prensa la Libertad) / 183 t: Matt Beardsell. Anthony Smith / 183 c: Benjamin Koh Ju Ren / 183 b: Waterfall overlay printed on Staufen PVC Gloss clear 220mig. Robert Horne Group Stardream swatch / 184 t: John Christenson—Nuzzles™ / 184 c: Photos, Art Direction, Designer: Miklos Kiss. Tire retailer and related services. Old building remodeled and rebuilt around the brand new concept, under a new name and a new brand. The special wall wrap is recycled tire (tiregranualted plate). General contractor: 7Fal Kft. Logo: T = service/O = tire retailer/O = tire control/B = car wash / 184 b: Fuse Collective/Peter Maciocha / 185 t, cl: Patrick Holmes/The Consult Design Ltd. / 185 cr: Ambush / 185 b: Design: Toko, Sydney / 186 tl: Fluid / 186 tr: Design and artwork by Marian Bantjes / 186 cr: Art Direction: Martin Pyper. Photography: Ruud Baan. Set Design: Gloudy & Sons and Me Studio / 186 bl, br: Design and Type: Me Studio. Photo: KDR Marcom and ID Laser / 187 t: Hans Gremmen / 187 bl: Designed, illustrated, and printed by John Magnifico / 187 br: Silkscreen, 118 x 84 cm, found at Wyber Zeefdruk, Amsterdam © Hans Gremmen and Wyber Zeefdruk 2008 / 188 l: Art Director: Marton Borzak. Graphic designers: Marton Borzak, Reka Diosi / 188 tr, cr, br: Engraving: Daniel Muntean. Photography: Daniel Muntean / 189: Kasper Pyndt. Jeppe Drensholt / 190: Szabó Balázs, Romania / 191: Graphic Designers: Daniele De Batté & Davide Sossi / 192: Aaron Alexander/Andy Cooke / 193: PANTONE Colors displayed herein may not match PANTONE-identified standards. Consult current PANTONE Color Publications for accurate color. PANTONE® and other Pantone trademarks are the property of, and are used with the written permission of, Pantone LLC. Portions © Pantone LLC, 2010. All rights reserved / 194 t, c: Work produced in response to a university brief based around scale, Aaron Alexander / 194 b: Lester Meachem / 195: Lester Meachem / 196: Die Reiter—"Visual Identity through Diversity" is the concept of a corporate design and album artwork for the German neopostmodern band "Die Reiter" / 197: Tristan O'Shannessy. Auckland University of Technology, Carolyn Kingscott / 198: Trapped in Suburbia / 200-201: Mission Design.